Joanne,
Interesting read~
Judy

W9-AYK-985

And
Justice for Some

An Exposé of the Lawyers and Judges
Who Let Dangerous Criminals Go Free

WENDY MURPHY

Wild Birch

Copyright 2007, Wendy Murphy
All rights reserved

Revised second edition published by Wild Birch Books, 2013.
www.wildbirchbooks.com
wildbirchbooks@gmail.com

ISBN: 978-1481849678

First published by Sentinel,
a member of Penguin Group (USA) Inc.,2007.

LIBRARY OF CONGRESS
CATALOGING IN PUBLICATION DATA

Murphy, Wendy, 1960-

And justice for some: an expose of the lawyers and judges who let dangerous criminals go free/Wendy Murphy.

p. cm
Criminal justice, Administration of—United States. I. Title.
KF9223.Z9M87   2007
345.73'05—DC22   2007001919

Printed in the United States of America

Designed by Spring Hoteling Set in Adobe Garamond
Without limiting the rights under copyright reserved above, no
part of this publication may be reproduced, stored in or introduced
into a retrieval system, or transmitted, in any form or by any
means (electronic, mechanical, photocopying, recording or
otherwise), without the prior written permission of both the
copyright owner and the above published of this book.

The scanning, uploading, and distribution of this book via the
Internet or via any other means without the permission of the
publisher is illegal and punishable by law. Please purchase only
authorized electronic editions and do not participate in or
encourage electronic piracy of copyrightable materials. Your
support of the author's rights is appreciated.

*To all the victims, win or lose, who fought for justice.
And to the silent ones who didn't even try
because they had no faith.*

PROLOGUE

Do not read this book if you're squeamish or prefer to think only about the brighter side of life. Just put it down and walk away.

But if you're interested in why so many terrible things happen to people, especially children, and why our legal system is making things worse, not better, read on.

This will be painful to read. I understand the sentiment. But we have to face our discomfort if we want our world to be a safer place, especially for kids.

The wonder of democracy is that it not only allows us, but invites us to become a part of the solution. That's what this book is about. It's filled with ideas that we can use to make our legal system better.

The language is harsh at times, but please don't mistake aggression for arrogance. I tried for twenty years to be polite. I shook many trees before figuring out that real change means tearing trees out by their roots.

Polite just doesn't work. It's that simple, and it's why I didn't use much flowery language and false modesty in this book. My words are direct, and at times demanding. Please don't be offended. I simply want the message to sound urgent.

If you're ready for a book like this, you will be transformed. My hope is that whatever you feel about the words on these pages, you will allow yourself to know and to face the truth. If that's the only thing that happens, I will have done what I set out to do, and it will have been worth it.

CONTENTS

FOREWORD

Most of us have heard the term "crusader for justice," and that is what Wendy Murphy is. Trying to reform the American justice system so that regular folks have a shot at some kind of fair play is a full-time job; one that is frustrating, sometimes maddening. The no-spin reason is that the United States is no longer a country that can tout "and justice for all." Now the legal system is Las Vegas, a game of chance, a roll of the dice. Even if you have been gravely wronged, the system may let you down big time. That's why you need to read this book.

Money, of course, is the root of all legal evil. The more you can spend, the more lawyers you can hire, the more "experts" you can buy to tell the jury things that will bewilder them, and the more private investigators you can hire to dig up dirt on your legal opponents. But if you are short of cash, watch out. The legal system is not a place where the poor are well accommodated.

So the deck is stacked from the start. Wealthy Americans have a much greater chance not only to get justice, but also to avoid justice. In a country that has declared "all men are created equal," there is something deeply disturbing about that.

In the upcoming pages, Wendy Murphy will walk us through what the American justice system has devolved into. She will introduce us to judges intoxicated by power, lawyers who put money above honesty, and jurors who just want to go home and will violate their consciences to do so. But the book also offers solutions and a call for reform. I mean, what kind of country are we if we allow children and the elderly to be brutalized with little consequence; if we accept a legal system that has allowed itself to spiral out of control so that its participants can get rich and powerful?

Through my thirty years in journalism, I have witnessed, pardon the pun, the decline of our justice system, and it must stop. We need reform from top to bottom. We need transparency, where folks can see the corrupt judges and greedy lawyers, and witness their fellow citizens being legally blackmailed or railroaded.

One of my favorite parts of Wendy Murphy's book is her anger at the so-called restorative justice idea, which has taken root in Vermont and Minnesota. I call this "wind-chime" jurisprudence. The basic premise is that for a crime to be fully adjudicated, everyone involved must be "healed." Of course, that includes the criminal who is not to be severely punished for his violation, but rehabilitated so that he realizes he must be nicer in the future. Somewhere very warm, Al Capone is grinning.

Restorative justice, the promulgation of unscrupulous tactics, lying to the media, and other modern legal techniques, are all analyzed and scorched by Wendy Murphy, who uses her pen like a blowtorch. If only the mercenary lawyers, corrupt judges, a deceitful press, and all the others who have made the courthouse a dangerous place, would adopt a sense of fairness and a knowledge of right and wrong.

The first step toward any reform is an exposition of the corruption. This book does that about as well as it can be done. It gets under the legal mumbo jumbo and offers you, the reader, strategies to avoid getting your head kicked in, if, God forbid, you wind up in a courtroom. It also offers a challenge to the powerful in America: Reform our legal system or admit it's a farce.

In her remarkable career as attorney and child advocate, Wendy Murphy has accomplished much, including chasing numerous bad guys down and holding them accountable. She has comforted the afflicted and annoyed the oppressors. She has stood for good and challenged evil in a way that is both vivid and effective.

In my opinion, *And Justice for Some* is her towering achievement. I am honored to be able to introduce it to you.

Bill O'Reilly
Long Island, New York
February 11, 2007

INTRODUCTION

You Call This Justice???

Let's open with a true horror story.

A man in Vermont named Mark Hulett raped a little girl countless times over a four-year period, beginning when she was only seven years-old. Sometimes he brought a buddy along, and they violated the child together. In 2005, Hulett was caught, tried, and convicted of the hideous crimes, to which he ultimately confessed. The prosecutor sought a sentence of eight to ten years.

The judge in the case, Edward Cashman, sentenced the rapist to just *sixty days in prison*.

Explaining his decision to an astonished courtroom, Judge Cashman said that when he was first elevated to the bench a quarter-century earlier, he believed in tough sentencing. More recently, though, he had concluded that being hard-nosed with bad guys did not serve any useful purpose. "It doesn't make anything better," he said. "It costs us a lot of money, we create a lot of expectation, and we feed on anger."

Let's stop right there, for a minute. How do you feel about that? Sixty days for four years of relentless rape and sexual abuse of a helpless child because being "hard-nosed

1

doesn't serve any useful purpose"?! There's a big difference between being "hard-nosed" toward a criminal and coddling him like he's an adolescent who stole a pack of gum! What's the obvious message to all the sex offenders lurking out there? What about the offender in *your* neighborhood?

When Fox News's Bill O'Reilly exposed Cashman on his show, O'Reilly showed the judge's picture and told his audience: "You may be looking at the worst judge in the U.S."

I agree that Cashman's in the running, although he has much competition for the title. And guess what: It's not only the judges we have to worry about. There are countless defense attorneys out there who are equally willing – probably even *more* willing – to put *you* at risk of harm by dishonoring the rule of law and the right of all law-abiding citizens to live in a safe world where dangerous criminals aren't allowed to walk free in society.

Do I sound angry? I am. And I want *you* to get angry, too, because our legal system is a mess, and it's breeding cynicism, mistrust in the rule of law, vigilantism and outright chaos. Mass shootings have skyrocketed, sex crimes are epidemic, only 2% of rapists spend even one day behind bars, and at least five children die from abuse every day in this country. Only a small percentage of criminals are ever arrested, much less prosecuted successfully, and when they do land in prison for crimes like rape and domestic violence, the criminals get better meals and health care than the women and children they abused and left homeless when they became incarcerated.

When I was in law school, it was common to hear some version of the following: *We Americans have the best legal system in the world.* We don't hear this very much anymore. You know why? Because we *don't* have the best legal system in the world. We only have the best legal system if you're a criminal. We actually have one of the *worst* systems if you're a victim or a law-abiding citizen.

I wrote this book because I care about the law, and I've been a lawyer long enough to know that our Constitution wasn't designed to allow millions of innocent citizens to be victimized by violence with impunity while dangerous criminals avoid sanctions for their crimes. In the aftermath of the terrorist attacks of 9/11, we all paid a little more attention to the rule of law and public safety. With a revived common fear and concern for the well-being of all Americans, we came together as a nation in a way that has breathed new life into fundamental American values of peace and prosperity.

I want us to keep our attention focused on these basic principles and to be mindful of the words spelled out in simple yet poignant terms at the end of our national pledge to one another. It's a pledge we make as equal investors in a nation unafraid to fight for common beliefs that unite us despite the vast array of differences that distinguish us from one another: "...with liberty and justice for all." Let me repeat that last part, "justice for all."

Today, this pledge is being dishonored by our justice system. The terrible truth is that a growing number of lawyers and judges are causing profound injustices while the rest of us get indigestion as we watch one criminal after another walk away from his crimes scot-free. We've seen it too many times - some smug thug on the courthouse steps, crowing into the microphones and TV cameras, with a smirk-faced lawyer by his side.

"Criminal justice" these days doesn't mean prosecuting a criminal in a "just" way. Instead, it means indulging and coddling a criminal, often at the expense of an innocent victim. Sure, we should make sure criminals have fair trials, and we should have compassion for *some* of the people behind bars. *Some* of them have good hearts and wound up in a dire situation due to a combination of tough luck and very bad judgment. We should help a guy get back on track, if, at the end of the day, he has the potential to care about others.

But an awful lot of people who commit crimes don't give a damn about anyone else. Maybe it's because they were abused as children, or because nobody ever cared about them. (This is the explanation for criminal behavior more often than we'd like to think.) In some situations, a terrible thing happened that made a guy hate the world, and the rest of us have to pay the consequences when he lashes out.

Some say it doesn't matter why bad guys do what they do. I disagree. I believe that if we could do a better job intervening in the lives of troubled kids before they become lawbreaking adults, there would be far less crime, and we'd save a ton of money, too. But we've never dedicated enough resources to the well-being of kids, mainly because as a society, we're hopelessly shortsighted, and nearsighted. And we don't really think much about crime until it happens to us, or to someone we love, or until the media serves up a wayward celebrity for our entertainment.

The fact that we don't devote enough resources to prevention is no excuse for going soft on criminals when they get caught. In today's society, we live at close quarters. We need to feel secure in our ability to interact safely with one another. Watching a criminal suffer a tough punishment for his crime is a powerful reminder that civility matters and that each of us has both rights AND responsibilities – not just rights!

Let me say that a little more bluntly. Too many people in this country think the Bill of Rights is designed *only* to protect and enforce the rights of criminals. This is simply not true. Many provisions explicitly apply to "persons," and the Constitution itself expressly mandates an *ordered liberty* – not some sort of criminal chaos! Our Founding Fathers clearly intended that while we enjoy our hard-won freedoms, we must also exercise our Constitutional duty to be civilized to one another.

Unfortunately, our criminal justice system sends the exact opposite message by routinely giving criminals a pass on the "responsibilities" part, a get-out-of-jail-free card, if you will, while overemphasizing the "rights" side of the citizenship bargain.

I was first exposed to this corrupt reality as a young prosecutor. I came to my job as an idealist, but that didn't last long. In case after case, the message that I saw conveyed to the criminal was, *now that you've been caught, the system will kiss your butt.* True, you may go to prison if you're convicted which, by the way, is highly unlikely in the majority of criminal cases, but, even if you're among the unlucky few who *do* wind up in jail, you will almost never get the time you deserve, and you will usually get out ahead of schedule.

Meanwhile, between the time you're arrested for your crime and the day the judge finally sentences you, the system will bend over backwards not only to be fair, which is a good thing, but also to make you comfortable and make your victim miserable, which is a very bad thing.

For example, if you're charged with a crime in a state like Massachusetts, where I practice, you can do all sorts of harmful things to your victims. What am I talking about, you wonder? Well, you can use taxpayer dollars to hire a private investigator to harass your victim's family and friends. You can use the authority of the government's subpoena powers to conduct "fishing expeditions" into your victim's private medical files. And, in virtually every state in the union, not just liberal Massachusetts, a criminal can commit perjury by lying under oath about his innocence, and he'll never get in trouble. If a rape victim lies under oath, she's likely to go to jail, but if her attacker does the same thing, nothing happens.

This is embarrassing, frustrating, and dangerous. President Clinton was nearly thrown out of office for lying about a non-criminal sexual event, but murderers and rapists commit perjury *every day*, in courtrooms across this country, and the justice system does absolutely nothing about it! These are things that a citizen who hasn't committed a crime can't get away with.

One more time: If you *don't* commit a crime, you won't ever be handed public dollars to hire an investigator to harass crime victims, and you will go to jail if you lie in court. But if you rape someone and get caught, you can do both things, often on the public's dime.

Rather than doing something about it, the people in charge tell victims the system is tough, and the trial will be brutal. How can we possibly expect people to report crimes and testify in criminal cases? And, if crimes aren't reported and citizens don't testify, how can police and prosecutors have any hope of ensuring the public's safety?

It's hard to believe that we live in a nation where people who have been victimized by crime are then expected to tolerate *more* harm in the name of justice. Victims and witnesses who cooperate with the prosecution should be handed good-citizenship awards. Instead, they get a kick in the head.

Wasn't our pledge to one another, a promise of "justice for all"? Isn't justice supposed to mean truth and fairness? Justice for some – maybe. Justice for all – not a chance.

After more than twenty years in the system, I still see things getting much worse, and I'm sick to my stomach. I see judges giving child sex offenders probation. I see defense attorneys lying through their teeth, and even victims and witnesses succumbing to outright corruption. I see a system out of control, and it's creating chaos rather than ordered liberty.

One of the reasons things are so bad is that law-abiding citizens haven't paid enough attention to the problem. I can understand this head-in-the-sand mentality. Most decent people in society think crime is "someone else's problem" and, much of the time, it is. But while the good guys aren't paying attention, the bad guys are taking over and running the system into the ground. If things don't change soon, it may be too late to do anything about it. Then we'll all be in trouble.

People who obey the law don't like thinking about crime because it's scary to grapple with the reality of human beings doing hideous things to each other. Again, I understand this mindset. Even after decades in the ugly business of criminal justice, I continue to be horrified by man's inhumanity. A young mother was arrested a few years ago for murdering her own newborn child by *cooking her in the microwave!* There were no markings on the child's body, but an autopsy showed the baby's flesh had literally been "roasted" on the inside. Some crimes need a whole new level of hell for the offender.

But here's an even scarier reality: Our justice system not only isn't making us safer, *it's making us more vulnerable to crime.* If you prefer to live in a safe world where criminals are not in charge, then you should not be content with the way things are now. More importantly, you should personally get involved and make things better. It's in your pledge. If you have declared your allegiance to a nation that promises "justice for all" then you have a duty as a citizen to help out when the system is promoting justice only for "some."

Writing this book has been difficult for me, and reading it will probably be tough for you. I think about cases where jurors acquitted an obviously guilty child rapist, not because the evidence was insufficient, but because they just couldn't believe that a man could commit a horrible act of violence against an adorable little three-year-old girl.

Jurors who can't handle the truth will vote "not guilty" every time simply because it makes them feel better. In that spirit of willful ignorance, some people who read this book may not be able to accept the ugly truth because it will be too painful.

Like you, I want to believe in the goodness of people. As the mother of five kids, it feels a whole lot better to me when I assume the world is *not* a dangerous place for them. But the sad reality is, crime happens all the time, and we are all at risk. Sexual violence, in particular, occurs with astounding frequency. It's hard to find an adult who *wasn't* sexually assaulted at some point in his or her life. Ask around. Listen hard. And don't be surprised by the answers.

This book is full of stories that will make you feel angry, sad, shocked, and, perhaps, even terrified. Please don't turn away. The truth is too important. The very justice system that claims to be keeping us safe is, instead, giving away the store to criminals and beating the figurative hell out of innocent victims. Worse than that, the judges and lawyers whom we count on to serve as guardians of the system, the so-called "officers of the court" are responsible for most of the trouble.

I tried fighting for change as a prosecutor, but after one too many judges told me my job was to "state the law, not complain about it," I gave up. I became a lawyer for victims in the real world where I would be free to speak the truth and fight for change.

I had two kids by the time I decided to leave the prosecutor's office. This personal reality made my professional decision much easier. As a young mother, I'd grown tired of telling other parents the shocking truth that the system cared much more about monstrous criminals than innocent children. Day after day, the cases came to me, and the staggering number of kids being brutalized was tearing my heart out. It was getting hard to go home every night and see my toddlers' trusting faces. Was all the time I was spending putting people behind bars for hurting kids making a difference? Could my children possibly be safe in such a scary world?

I was lucky enough to have excellent daycare. My dad's sister cared for my children, and she could not have been more loving and protective. But in the pile of cases on my desk, I could see that parents *just like me* were discovering every day that their kids had been hurt by someone they trusted, someone they believed was a loving caregiver.

One day, I asked my two-year-old son what he had done that day at Auntie's. In his loud but imprecise little voice, he replied, "I eat Tom's penis." If you're a parent, you know exactly how I felt. I nearly passed out. After composing myself, I started asking questions, non-leading ones as any good prosecutor should: "What room were you in?" "Was Auntie there?" "What was Tom doing?" When I asked this last question, my son replied, "He pick up da shells on da floor." I started laughing. My precious little boy had been eating Tom's peanuts. All was well! But during that endless split second, when I was thinking the worst, I realized something terrible. I realized that I, as someone who understood the system and could make sure it was as fair as possible, did not want my own child to endure the burdens of an unfair system.

This meant, in turn, that absolutely nothing would be done in my child's (imaginary) case. I soon realized it was time to stop killing myself inside a badly broken system, where the criminals were laughing and the good guys were crying. As a prosecutor, there was little I could do to make things better. But if I left the district attorney's office, maybe I could make a *real difference*.

Twenty years later, I wrote this book because I *have* made a difference. I've had real success – satisfying, gratifying success - fighting for victims, and I want to share my strategies with you, so that you can help, too.

But before you can get involved, you have to understand how the system works and why things are so badly broken. It's essential for you to learn as much as you can so that you can participate effectively in public discussions about criminal justice matters and become a great advocate for a better legal system.

This book will help you fight back. It will give you insight into why terrible things happen to innocent people all the time, and it will let you in on some of the dirty tricks and evil tactics that undermine the integrity of our justice system. Read it and weep – but don't stop there.

Do something!

ONE

Murphy's Law, Rewritten

You've heard of Murphy's Law. It's the one that
says, "If something can go wrong, it will go wrong, at the
worst possible moment."

I propose to rewrite Murphy's Law. From now on, I
want (Wendy) Murphy's Law to read, "It can't go wrong if
people like you and me don't let it."

Before you can buy that rewrite, though, you need to
know a little more about me.

In the past two decades, I've been a prosecutor, a law
professor at New England Law l Boston, a lecturer at the
Massachusetts Institute of Technology, a Visiting Scholar at
Harvard Law School, and a legal analyst for CBS News,
MSNBC, CNN and Fox News.

For what it's worth, I've appeared as a legal expert
on virtually every major network and cable news show. I've
also served as an editor and writer for a national anti-
violence publication and Women's eNews, and I've written
columns for the *Daily Beast*, the *Boston Herald* and the *Patriot
Ledger*.

I was, for many years, assistant district attorney in
Massachusetts, where I specialized in child abuse and sex

crimes cases. As an attorney in private practice, I've sued powerful institutions, and written dozens of appellate briefs in state and federal courts around the country, including the United States Supreme Court. Many of my cases have changed the law to better protect the rights of crime victims. I've published numerous academic and law review articles and book chapters. I've worked with Congress and state legislatures and consulted on cases affecting the lives of women and children around the world. I even took on Harvard, Princeton, and the University of Virginia (among many other schools) when they violated the rights of women under Title IX by treating victims of sex crimes on campus unfairly.

As a matter of fact, I was the first lawyer in the country to start forcing schools to apply Title IX to sexual assault cases. Even today, most school administrators think of Title IX as requiring equality for women in sports, but Title IX does apply to all forms of gender discrimination, including sexual harassment; the most serious expression of which is sexual assault.

When Harvard adopted a rule in 2002 requiring "independent corroboration" in sexual assault cases, essentially declaring that the word of a woman wasn't good enough, the students started protesting, and they asked me for legal help. I'd been waiting for a good test case that I could use to put pressure on schools to treat violence against women as a civil rights problem under Title IX, so I filed a complaint against the ivy league institution with the Department of Education's Office for Civil Rights. We won the landmark case and not only was Harvard forced to withdraw the offensive policy, but also, schools everywhere started changing their sexual assault rules to comport with Title IX. Things have been getting better ever since, because when Harvard gets in trouble everyone notices.

I also prevailed against the military when a victim's civilian rape counselor was ordered to turn over her treatment file in a case where a guy from the Air Force Academy was being court-martialed for rape. As the attorney for the counselor, I instructed my client not to comply with the order because the military had no power over civilian psychotherapists. I submitted a brief to the judge explaining the law and making it clear to him that he had no authority to compel the release of the victim's privileged treatment file. The judge did not care about the law. He ruled against us and threatened to have my client arrested.

We still refused to comply and the judge issued an arrest warrant and sent federal law enforcement officers to my client's home. I dared them to arrest her and promised a swift and expensive lawsuit if they took her into custody. A group of government lawyers had an emergency meeting in D.C. and told the U.S. Marshall I was right. The officers were instructed to stand down.

When the military judge in Texas learned that federal officials refused to enforce his arrest warrant, he flipped out. Some time later, that judge was reassigned.

My client's bold resistance inspired many military rape victims to fight harder for justice, and things are getting better, but we have a long way to go to protect servicewomen from abuse.

I file cases like the ones against Harvard and the military all the time. I've sued hospitals, au pair agencies, nursing homes, defense attorneys, and even state court judges when they violate my clients' federal Constitutional rights.

I've served on numerous boards and commissions, given a zillion keynote speeches to thousands of people across the country, and worked my butt off representing crime victims, mostly for free.

In between, I gave birth to five children, all of whom have come to court with me as babies or toddlers when I had no choice. My youngest made her debut at the

Massachusetts Supreme Judicial Court at the ripe old age of two and a-half days. My children have been raised by two parents and the world's best babysitter, Sandy, and while they didn't like it that I was always working so hard, they've grown into compassionate young adults who give of themselves generously to serve to the less fortunate.

What else? I have a closet full of awards. I've been named "Activist Mother of the Year" by *Glamour* magazine, and "Lawyer of the Year" in Massachusetts. I received the first-ever award for outstanding advocacy for crime victims from the National Crime Victim Law Institute, not only for developing new ideas and practices, but also for pushing the justice system relentlessly to make it work better for the good guys.

I'm not telling you all this to boast. I'm not really a boastful type at all, although I think women, in particular, too often shy away from talking about the good work they do even as the men around them don't think twice (nor should they) before talking about how they closed a big business deal or signed up a big client.

I'm telling you all this because I am proud to fight for victims and because I want you to know I speak from experience. I also want you to realize that if I can make a difference so can you. We need to support each other and talk proudly about what we do because too many people who work hard in this fight every day toil in isolation. Most prosecutors, for example, regularly put in more than a full work week, but they get little of what I call "cultural self-esteem," the feeling that what they do, for very little pay, is appreciated by the public. I want that to change.

People who fight for victims need more support because, unlike the fight for criminals' rights, victims are not part of the political machine. There's no big clanking infrastructure for victims, supported by influential ideologues and special interest groups. And, it's a tough job to do psychologically. Dealing with unimaginable horrors every day makes it nearly impossible to go home and act like a "normal" human being or have ordinary conversations with neighbors about work. I've gotten to the point where when people ask me at dinner parties what kind of work I do, I warn them in advance before I respond.

But I keep at it because I believe I have a responsibility to help people who are suffering and to promote the true meaning and integrity of the word "justice."

So, when you come across someone doing this kind of work, thank him or her. If you are already helping out, thank you. And if you meet someone doing harm to the system, let them know how you feel.

It used to infuriate me to hear mean-spirited jokes about attorneys, but not anymore! I've grown disgusted with too many of my colleagues, the lawyers and lawyers-turned-judges, who bring shame to my profession by lying, cheating, and manipulating the system to cause unjust results.

Contrary to the nonsense we heard from defense attorneys after the O. J. Simpson debacle, when dangerous criminals are allowed to walk around free in society, it's absolutely *not* good for democracy. Simpson's acquittal was revolting. Yet people in my profession actually cheered when they heard the verdict, as they often do when a guilty criminal wins. When lawyers win unjust acquittals by exploiting racism or by hiring experts to testify (for a price) that, "Twinkies made him do it," they high-five each other as if disrespecting the system is something to celebrate!

To make matters worse, most ex-prosecutors become defense attorneys; and when they switch sides, they no longer have an incentive to fight the injustices and dirty tricks. Rather, they start using the dirty tricks themselves to win cases. I could have become a defense attorney, but I stayed on the victims' side of things when I left the prosecutor's office because I knew it was important to have a former insider speaking openly about the scandalous problems that plague our justice system.

Criminals get a lot if sympathy when they complain about unfair treatment, but how much is ever said about the mistreatment of victims and law-abiding citizens? How many of you are even aware of a recent study that found one in five of you will become a crime victim and nearly half of those victimized won't report the crime to police? Theories abound about why this is so, but what I hear every day is that people don't believe in the system anymore. It isn't "worth it" they say because the process is slow, painful, and too often ends with an unjust result. Criminals don't feel this way, but victims and law-abiding citizens do. Criminals are having a field day generating big news stories about how the system is unfair, while the truth is that they're being coddled. It's the victims who are being harmed!

When a story broke a few years ago about a public defender who fell asleep in court, it made front-page headlines, advocated for criminals, and called for large-scale reforms. But, when swaths of victims are denied access to justice, there are no headlines.

This disparity in treatment is important not only because how we administer justice matters, but also because the public has a right to know how and when their money is being wasted. Our court system is paid for by tax dollars, which means everything that happens is, to some extent, controlled by the American people. We have a right to know how our money is being spent, and if the system is using our money to cause harm to innocent people. We have a right to demand change.

One way our money is being wasted is on taxpayer-funded lawyers for criminals who aren't really poor. Soon after pedophile priest John Geoghan became the focus of a criminal investigation in Massachusetts for sexually abusing little boys, he transferred his interest in two properties to his sister for one dollar. One of the homes was an oceanfront estate. By the time he needed an attorney to represent him at trial, he claimed to be indigent. This got him a lawyer paid for by the public. He should have been forced to rescind his fraudulent transfer of wealth and at least pay something for an attorney. Instead, the taxpayers paid a small fortune to help the predatory molester try to escape justice. Geoghan virtually stole money away from truly poor defendants who legitimately needed publicly funded lawyers to protect their rights.

If there were better oversight of public defenders' budgets, fraud could be prevented and more money would be available for all sorts of things to help the system work better, like more legal protection for the rights of victims.

I'm not saying that all victim's rights are equal in weight to all defendant's rights, but more should be done when the personal and Constitutional rights of victims are threatened or violated. Prosecutors can't help because they represent the state, and the state has a responsibility to protect the rights of the accused. In other words, that prosecutor isn't really on the victim's side; he or she is on everybody's side.

I'm glad prosecutors protect the rights of criminals, but that leaves nobody to advocate for the victim, and without a voice, victims' struggles are invisible.

Family Justice Centers help a little bit. They offer victims "one-stop shopping" where they can get access to law enforcement and community-based services under one roof. This approach helps victims stay connected to the legal system, which increases the likelihood that justice will be served.

There are a few problems, however.

First, these centers exist in only a few states.

Second, most Family Justice Centers don't provide lawyers, and even if they did, the fact that they receive federal funds means the lawyers would be largely ineffective. Government-funded lawyers for victims are severely limited in the work they do and can't, for example, file appeals when a victim's rights are violated, or speak out in the press against an unfair decision of a judge. So, Family Justice Centers are O.K., but to make the system work fairly for victims, much more needs to be done.

For example, victims need more opportunities to speak out publicly or to have others speak out for them when injustice happens. Let's face it, we live in a media world. When it comes to holding the system accountable, there's nothing better than a powerful TV appearance. I don't know how many times during the Michael Jackson trial I found myself screaming at a defense attorney on television for saying something like: "The fact that Michael Jackson sleeps with little boys doesn't mean he's a pedophile." The victim couldn't speak out because he was a child, and the trial was still pending. But Jackson's defenders were all over the news shows and were having a tremendous influence over public sentiment. It was important for the victim, and for the child advocates, to have their voices heard, too. Bill O'Reilly understood this better than most and often had guests like me on his show, *The O'Reilly Factor,* so we could speak for the kids.

This is important work, and I'm glad to be able to be a voice for victims on television. We all have to speak up in whatever venues we have because we are all part of public oversight, and together, we can provide immeasurable benefits to the integrity of the system simply by taking the time to notice and to *say something* when injustice happens.

I'm not suggesting that every judicial decision should be influenced by opinion polls. An independent judiciary is important, and public opinion is sometimes wrong. But it is essential that the public's perspective be brought to bear on the definition of "justice" because it is a core idea around which society is organized. Judges and prosecutors are supposed to take the victim's and the public's opinion into account when they make discretionary decisions. But, too often, those viewpoints are ignored, simply because the people in charge assume that nobody is watching.

We have to show them that we are watching.

Media celebrities like Bill O'Reilly may not effect changes in the law in quite the same way as when a brilliant brief is filed in court. But sometimes standing up for victims on television has a huge affect because there's no defense attorney or judge complaining that the victim has "no right to be heard." I hear this all the time when I show up in criminal court on behalf of a victim. I wish I had a dime for every brief I've written on the issue of "victim standing to be heard" in criminal cases.

I understand why it makes people nervous when a victim shows up with her own lawyer. When I was a prosecutor, and it happened in my cases, I worried that the lawyer might mess up the trial. But things are so out of control now, with defense lawyers being allowed unprecedented authority to hurt victims in the name of justice, the system has no choice but to allow victims to be represented by private lawyers to help put a stop to the suffering.

I wouldn't be fighting as hard as I do if judges did a better job prohibiting defense attorneys from using the criminal justice process to cause even more harm to victims, but so long as the behavior is allowed to continue, I will fight back.

This book is a call to arms. It is a shout-out to you and to all those who think the way we do justice is important, even if you never step one foot inside a courtroom. Why do I inject myself into criminal cases on behalf of victims? Because I want the world I live in to be a place that cares about fairness, and where truth matters. I want the people who suffer to have a voice, and I want our kids to grow up believing that fairness in our legal system matters. If we really want our legal system to inspire civility and mutual respect, we have to hold our legal system accountable when chaos, corruption and dirty tricks rule the courthouse. The American people will not long respect a system that turns a blind eye to the suffering of innocent victims in the name of justice.

Fighting against injustice isn't easy. I've often told people that for me, it's like climbing a mountain of ice while wearing plastic slippers. It's cold, I don't get much traction, and the surface is solid and relentlessly unforgiving. But I keep on climbing because that's what it takes to tackle such a big problem. The more of us who tackle the mountain, in one way or another, the faster we will melt the ice and see the benefits of a more fair distribution of justice, like safer streets, fewer school shootings, less online sexual exploitation of children, longer prison sentences, treatment for all criminals during incarceration, better judicial accountability, and, ultimately, more compassion and human kindness.

At the beginning of this chapter, I proposed a rewrite of Murphy's Law to get us out of a defeatist mindset and on track for success. Now that we've covered some of the basics, it's time for the tough stuff. We can't fix anything without first getting a handle on the dirty tricks that provide the foundation for what's wrong with our legal system. Most of the ugliness goes unnoticed, and people like you rarely complain, not because you don't care, but because you haven't yet been let in on the secrets.

Let the unveiling begin.

T W O

Manufacturing Innocence with DNA Lies

Let's get one thing on the table right away. There's nothing wrong with zealous advocacy for accused criminals. Public relations people are paid to spin, and lawyers are paid to advocate. The more energetically they do it, assuming they have the necessary smarts and skills, the more favorable the results.

Zealous advocacy is what great lawyers do. It's perfectly fair to try to persuade a judge or jury or the public to see things in a certain light. But lying about evidence is not spin or advocacy, it's fraud. One of the biggest frauds being perpetrated in the criminal justice system today is the claim that some two hundred convicted criminals have been declared innocent as a result of new DNA tests on old cases. The truth is that most of the criminals whose convictions have been overturned because of new DNA tests are not *innocent*. Read those stories and listen to the news reports carefully. The word they use is "exonerated." What the stories don't tell you is that a person can be legally "exonerated" and, at the same time, one hundred percent factually "guilty." This means that many of the claims of defense lawyers are misleading if not outright false.

No, this is not a criticism of all, or even many, defense attorneys. The vast majority of lawyers who defend criminals are honest people, sincere in their advocacy for clients they don't even like. It makes me proud of my profession that lawyers are willing to represent dangerous and evil people because it takes a lot of courage, discipline, and commitment to the core values of a free society to stand next to a monster and insist that he deserves to be set free, even if guilty, because the government didn't prove its case. This is a noble thing to do, period. I won't even add any qualifications about how the worst thugs shouldn't get the best possible representation. Thugs deserve due process; and defense attorneys deserve kudos for making sure we adhere to this important principle.

Defense attorneys deserve extra points, many extra points, for being the heroes of the truly innocent men who have been unjustly convicted. In several cases, the dogged efforts of defense counsel have led to the discovery of old evidence in dusty files; evidence that, when submitted for DNA testing, proved scientifically that a man previously convicted of a crime was completely innocent. It's heartening to watch news clips of innocent men being released from prison and running into the waiting arms of loved ones. The media pounces on these stories with alacrity. It's wonderful stuff.

The problem is that we have no way of knowing how many exonerated individuals are   guilty, and how many had nothing to do with the crime of which they were convicted. In a January 23, 2007, Associated Press story, a reporter cited lawyers at the Innocence PrO.J.ect as claiming 194 men have been exonerated through DNA tests, but there was nothing in the story about what "exonerated" means or even a suggestion that it does not mean factually innocent. Often, defense attorneys and the media claim (or falsely imply) that an individual has been proven innocent by new DNA tests. In a May 5, 2004, *Boston Herald* story on wrongful convictions, the reporter wrote, "Throughout the country 143 *innocent* suspects have been freed since 1990" [emphasis mine]. Misleading use of the word "exoneration" is one thing, but calling them all "innocent suspects" is an outright lie.

Exoneration is a catchall word that comprises a range of possible meanings, including that the person is factually guilty. This is because "exonerated" could mean that the person's conviction was overturned, and he or she wasn't retried because the witnesses had long since died or were unavailable, or the suspect had served his whole sentence before the new DNA tests were conducted. That a conviction was overturned and a criminal was not retried does *not* mean the person who was convicted did not commit the crime. It simply means the legal system did not find him guilty. This is the same judgment that was reached in the O.J. Simpson case. Would you call him innocent?

The public has a right and a need to know the truth about which cases involve actual innocence and which cases involve a clearly guilty criminal using the development of new DNA technology to win a new trial. It matters a lot if new DNA tests do nothing but muddy the waters with tangential or barely relevant evidence to help get a criminal out of jail on a scientific technicality.

Defense attorneys don't mind that the word "exonerated" is misunderstood to mean actual innocence because they benefit from the confusion. Many of them have been gaining political power, and winning boatloads of money, by suing the government on behalf of exonerated-but-guilty criminals. Clearly, this business venture would be far less lucrative if the distinction weren't so blurry. Why? Because representing a guilty man who was properly convicted but just happened to get off, not because he's innocent, or even because the government did something wrong, but because DNA science wasn't around at the time of his trial doesn't make for much of a lawsuit. But representing a man the public believes is totally innocent is worth a hell of a lot of more. It's no wonder clever lawyers try to make the former situation look like the latter one by using murky terminology like "exonerated."

The American public should be outraged that hundreds of millions of tax dollars are wasted settling lawsuits on behalf of exonerated-but-factually-guilty men. Our money is being delivered in ribbon-wrapped wheelbarrows to murderers and rapists who actually committed their crimes v.

Shouldn't we at least be keeping track of how the public's money is being spent in these cases? Shouldn't someone be checking to see whether government officials are paying excessive and quick settlements, not because a completely innocent man spent half his life in prison (which deserves compensation), but because it's the politically expedient thing to do?

The media bear some of the blame for this fiasco because it is difficult to find a reporter willing to write about the difference between exonerated and innocent. Conversely, it's all too easy to find people willing to parrot false but oft-repeated misleading claims like "more than 150 innocent men have been cleared through new DNA tests." Exonerated, yes; innocent, no.

But it gets worse. Certain reporters are only too eager to ignore facts that work against the interests of the guilty. Take the simple fact that sex offenders have a disproportionately high recidivism rate. ("Recidivism" means committing additional offenses after the first one.) Benjamin Radford, a reporter for a bimonthly magazine called the *Skeptical Enquirer*, wrote in 2006 that assertions of high recidivism rates for sex offenders were false and little more than fear-mongering. Furthermore, Radford claimed that sex offenders have a lower recidivism rate than other criminals. To support his position, he cited federal data showing that "just 5 percent" of convicted sex offenders were rearrested for a sex crime in the three-year period after their release from prison. He said this proves that sex offenders are no more likely to reoffend than other types of criminals. "There seems little justification for the public's fear," he concluded.

But Radford conveniently neglected to mention that the federal data he cited looked only at rearrest rates, not reoffense rates. Given that 90 percent of child-sex crimes are never reported, much less lead to arrest, it hardly makes sense to declare anything about recidivism based on the numbers of times these perpetrators are rearrested. Radford also ignored research that emphasizes the importance of measuring recidivism by looking at long-term data. Three years is a woefully inadequate length of time in which to learn the truth about reoffense patterns for any particular sex offender. Here's the hard truth: Sex offenders are so damn sneaky, and so manipulative in causing their victims not to report the crime, they are almost never caught, much less arrested or prosecuted within three years. It is this extra fog of evil, rather than exemplary behavior upon release from prison, that explains the low recidivism rate in the federal study cited by Radford.

This isn't just my opinion; much research backs me up. When researchers study recidivism by asking offenders about their behavior, rather than by looking at arrest rates, the numbers are shocking. In her book *Predators*, Dr. Anna Salter cites one study involving convicted offenders who were asked how many victims they'd abused in their lifetime. When the men were instructed that they had to tell the truth in order to be released on parole, they revealed having molested an average of about a dozen victims each. When the same group was told they would be subjected to a polygraph examination to test their honesty, many changed their answers and said they'd victimized, on average, seventy victims each! Another study, funded by the

National Institute of Mental Health, found the average child molester abuses 117 victims over the course of his lifetime.

I wish Radford's poor reporting were an unusual case, but it isn't. The mainstream media spend far more energy writing nonsense about criminals and new DNA tests, while simultaneously turning a blind eye to the truth about what really happened to the victim. We all need to read these kinds of stories with a critical eye and an appropriate degree of skepticism.

I'm not saying we should doubt the power of DNA science to establish conclusively the identity of a person whose blood or other body fluid is found at a crime scene. But it's important to remember that:

1) Finding a particular person's DNA does not necessarily mean that he committed the crime; and

2) Not finding a particular person's DNA doesn't necessarily mean that he didn't.

One notorious example of the way DNA science has distorted the truth is the Central Park Jogger case, in which a young woman was brutally attacked in New York's Central Park and left for dead. Many young men committed the ghastly crime together, and five were convicted after confessing to the crime in detail and on videotape, four in the presence of parents or adult relatives. They subsequently claimed their confessions were coerced by police, but after a six-week hearing, the judge in the case found no evidence of coercion. The judge also noted that the perpetrators had confessed to friends or made other damning admissions *before* talking to cops and in circumstances that had nothing to do with police interrogations.

The five young men were interrogated separately, and their confessions were not only consistent with one another on key facts, they also included information that only someone who was present at the crime scene could have known. For example, one of the guys said the victim's

Walkman was stolen during the crime. He made this statement long before cops even knew the victim had been carrying a Walkman because the attack left her in a coma for months.

Years after the five men were convicted, a sixth man named Matias Reyes came forward and confessed to the crime. His semen was found on the victim's body using DNA technology that was unavailable at the time of the crime. Reyes told cops he acted alone. Did the absence of DNA from the other offenders mean they weren't involved? No, it only meant they didn't leave any strong biological evidence at the crime scene. Why would Reyes claim to have acted alone if it weren't true? It doesn't really matter although it's interesting that cops soon learned that when new DNA tests were being conducted, Reyes was serving time on other charges in the same prison as one of the five men who confessed (who was in prison on other crimes). The two prisoners discussed the case, and cops theorize that Reyes may have been threatened or offered something of value in exchange for falsely claiming to have committed the crime alone. No surprise, the five men who confessed went on to file a 250 million dollar wrongful conviction lawsuit against the city of New York!

Take another example, this one hypothetical, in which a drug addict who is indebted to his dealer agrees to kidnap and deliver a child to that dealer for sexual services as payment. Most likely, only the dealer would leave DNA on or in the child's body, but both would be equally guilty of the crime. Let's say, hypothetically, that multiple eyewitnesses to the crime saw the kidnapping of the child, but not the sexual assault. What if the man whose DNA was found years later then claimed that he acted alone? The defense would almost certainly argue that finding the DNA of the dealer on the child's body, and none from the kidnapper, proves the kidnapper's innocence – especially if the dealer says he acted alone.

Similar fact patterns have led to the release of countless exonerated-but-guilty criminals and have ended with murderers and rapists being handed millions of *our tax dollars* for their "wrongful" convictions.

The majority of these exoneration cases involve sexual violence against women and children, which means the very nature of the crime scene increases the risk of DNA's distortion power. The victim's underwear or genital area is a far more confined space than the crime scene of a murder (e.g., an entire room in a home, public park, or bar).

Considering that most sex crimes cases turn on the issue of consent, the presence or absence of DNA in a victim's body is either irrelevant or misleading on the question of guilt. And even if the identity of the perpetrator is unknown or disputed, the absence of DNA in the victim's body may reveal nothing about guilt or innocence because the perpetrator may have worn a condom or failed to complete the sex act. One recent study found that 50 percent of rapes end without ejaculation. Even if no condom is used and the victim is examined immediately after the incident, it is not unusual for medical experts to find no DNA in the victim's body.

In January 2007, a federal court upheld the 1999 New York conviction of Jermaine Barnes for raping a twelve-year-old girl. He ejaculated and did not use a condom. The child reported the crime immediately and was taken to the hospital where a rape kit examination was performed. Not only was there no DNA found that matched that of Mr. Barnes, the child's hymen was completely intact. Before you start wondering whether Mr. Barnes might be innocent, you need to know that he confessed to police in writing and on videotape. During a search of Barnes's home, police found the child's blood and Barnes's semen on the towel the guy used to wipe himself after the crime.

Clearly, the absence of DNA is *not* proof of innocence. Likewise, the presence of someone else's DNA may reveal nothing about the actual innocence of the person whose DNA was not found because the victim may have had consensual sex with someone else around the time of the crime. DNA can stay in the body for many days, and on undergarments for months - even after laundering! Just because the DNA is hearty, and the "crime scene" is small, doesn't mean we have reason to abandon common sense. But this is exactly what's happening in courtrooms, and by extension, in newspapers all over the country.

Another more sinister example of when DNA can be used to distort rather than elucidate the truth arises when a criminal intentionally plants someone else's DNA at the crime scene or on his own body to taint the evidence or falsely implicate an innocent person. Consider, for example, a recent New York case in which murder defendant Martin Heidgen was court-ordered to open his mouth so that police could obtain a buccal (lining-of-the-mouth) swab sample of his DNA for comparison to blood evidence found at the crime scene. The results came back "mixed," meaning that another man's DNA, as well as Heidgen's, was present. Police traced that extra DNA to a man whose semen was found inside the body of a victim from an old unsolved rape investigation.

The prosecutor said Heidgen "tried to thwart the test by mixing a sample." Defense lawyer Stephen LaMagna contended that the test had been mishandled by officials, and said it was absurd to blame it on his client. But the judge, obviously an old pro, noted that "it would be interesting if that other sample turned out to be a wanted sex offender presently incarcerated in the [same] jail" where Heidgen was being held.

Tampering with DNA evidence would lead to widespread public outrage if a cop or a prosecutor did it. Charges would be dismissed and lawsuits would be flying. Just Google the case of Massachusetts Crime Lab Technician Annie Dookhan (though read the stories with a healthy dose of skepticism). Most corrupt lab techs mess with evidence because they get paid off by drug dealers to replace heroin with baby powder and other innocuous substances. But guess what happens when a criminal or his lawyer messes with evidence? Nothing. That's right. No punishment. No lawsuit. No accountability for causing harm to the system, wasting resources, or even for falsely implicating an innocent man. Think about that. A thug who's been charged with a crime can plant someone else's DNA on a piece of evidence and cause a completely innocent man to be suspected or convicted of a crime he did not commit, and nothing happens to the thug - as if there's a Constitutional right to cause the wrongful persecution of an innocent person.

This is an increasingly serious problem for prosecutors and police considering popular television programs like *Law and Order* and the various *CSI*-type shows that hype up the value of DNA evidence. In turn, jurors in the real world develop irrational expectations and acquit clearly guilty criminals based on some nutty idea they saw on a television crime show.

Memo to Hollywood: Thanks a lot.

There is room for hope, however, because one man with the power to make a difference is starting to shine an antiseptic light on this charade. Josh Marquis, the District Attorney of Clatsop County, Oregon, and past vice president of the National District Attorneys' Association, explains why he has put so much of his own time and energy into exposing this fraud:

> My passion has been fueled by a thirst for honesty in the debate about these important issues. It is an outright lie to call a killer or rapist "innocent" or even "exonerated" simply because a judge reversed a conviction after new DNA evidence indicated the presence of an unknown person at the crime scene,

but a new trial was not possible because victims and witnesses were unable or unavailable to testify. And frankly, it cheapens the significance of those rare cases where an individual was proved factually innocent by new DNA tests. The worst part of the problem is that these fraudulent stories make people think prisons are chock full of doe-eyed innocents, and that is pure urban legend.

Marquis has written and lectured extensively on what he calls the "myth of innocence." He agrees with me that holding even one innocent person on death row is unacceptable. At the same time, he notes that even people who are actively opposed to the death penalty, such as Judge Jed S. Rackoff of the U.S. District Court, Southern District of New York, agree that the number of innocent men who were ever on death row at any time in history probably amounts to no more than thirty. Others note that no factually innocent person has ever been executed despite the oft-quoted erroneous claim that hundreds of innocent men have languished on death row, and that many have been executed.

Marquis is guardedly optimistic that things are getting better in terms of the public's understanding of the truth, and he points to the United States Supreme Court as proof. In its recent *Kansas v. Marsh* decision, the Court cited Marquis's work detailing the stories of two killers on death row, both of whom received widespread publicity in support of their claims of innocence. One of them, Ricky McGinn, even appeared on the cover of *Newsweek*, and the accompanying article hinted broadly at his probable innocence.

McGinn had been convicted in 1995 of raping and murdering his twelve-year-old stepdaughter, Stephanie Flannery, though earlier forensic tests had been unable to identify the source of a biological sample found in the child's underpants. McGinn's lawyers convinced then-Governor George W. Bush of Texas to grant McGinn a reprieve from death row so that new DNA tests could be conducted on some of the evidence found at the crime scene. In June 2000, DNA test results came back conclusively proving that McGinn had both raped and murdered the child. Did the reconfirmed truth about his guilt make the cover of *Newsweek*? You know the answer: It did not.

One thing to keep in mind is that guilty people can often persuade themselves, at least in some corner of their brain, that they're innocent – and that makes them very persuasive. A typical example comes from my home state of Massachusetts, and involves a man named Ben LaGuer, convicted in 1984 of raping an elderly woman over an eight-hour period. In 2002, LaGuer insisted that DNA would prove his innocence. After much celebratory media coverage and support from lawyers like Barry Sheck and influential public figures like the late former president of Boston University, John Silber, and Massachusetts Governor Deval Patrick, new DNA tests were conducted. They confirmed LaGuer's guilt beyond all doubt.

LaGuer continued to falsely protest his innocence with intensity, and at last count he had filed his ninth appeal. Some people believe LaGuer's persistence is evidence of his innocence. But consider that the same narcissistic and sociopathic tendencies that lead people to commit horrendous crimes in the first place may well propel them to relentlessly protest their innocence. Maybe even stranger than LaGuer's persistence is the fact that lawyers, including James Rehnquist, son of the former chief justice of the United States Supreme Court, continue to stand up for the guy. I'll always be open to the possibility that a convicted criminal is telling the truth when he passionately proclaims his innocence, but what I want to know is why so many seemingly smart people find it so darned difficult to consider the far more likely possibility that he's guilty.

How do lawyers get sucked into these cases? Are they so blinded by anti-prosecution ideology that they don't mind spending hundreds of hours of pro bono time helping an obviously guilty killer go free, even after a fair trial and many failed appeals? Maybe for James Rhenquist, it's some kind of rebellion against his father's uber-conservative philosophy. I don't know – but it's weird.

Remember Martin Heidgen, the accused murderer who allegedly took DNA from a fellow prisoner and put it into his own mouth so he could mess up the evidence when cops took a saliva sample? Heidgen might have heard about a similar trick Ben LaGuer tried decades earlier, a trick no doubt shared among countless criminals and their lawyers over the years. Like Heidgen, LaGuer was in jail awaiting trial when police got a court order to take a swab of the inside of his mouth. They wanted to compare LaGuer's saliva to evidence found at the scene (they couldn't conduct DNA tests back then because it was 1983 and the technology hadn't yet been developed, but they could do certain tests on saliva that were more sensitive than blood type testing, alone). LaGuer knew what police were planning to do, so he literally took bodily fluid from a fellow prisoner and mixed it in with his own saliva so that when the swab was taken, police got a mixed result. Would an innocent man try to contaminate his own saliva with the biological fluid of another prisoner to contaminate the test results? You know the answer.

Not long after the LaGuer case was in the news, CNN highlighted the case of Derek Barnabei, a man convicted in 1995 of murdering a woman named Sara Winsosky. Barnabei's supporters claimed that fingernail scrapings from the victim that had not previously been tested would prove Barnabei's innocence. However, tests in 2000 proved the opposite - that Barnabei was guilty. Again, this confirmatory outcome didn't generate nearly as much news coverage as the original (false) claims that the guy was innocent.

Another case that received little truthful attention involves a man named Kerry Kotler. Kotler was one of the first and most celebrated cases of the Innocence PrO.J.ect. According to test results from a defense expert, Kotler was innocent of a rape for which he had previously been convicted. The Innocence PrO.J.ect successfully championed Kotler's release from prison in 1992, and then won a financial settlement of $1.5 million for his "wrongful conviction." Soon after Kotler was set free, he committed a similar horrific crime. Needless to say, representatives from the Innocence PrO.J.ect do not like talking about the Kotler case. (Their website tersely claims that: "He would later be convicted of different charges on the basis of DNA evidence.")

You won't be surprised to learn that the media paid little attention to Kotler's new arrest and conviction, especially compared to the mountains of press attention that followed his "wrongful conviction." Such disparities in news coverage might not be a big deal if they didn't cause such a serious public safety problem. When exonerated-but-guilty men, especially prolific criminals such as sex offenders, are released and mischaracterized as *innocent*, the public is unaware of the need to be vigilant to protect themselves and their children from harm. The exonerated-but-guilty status allows these guys to walk around completely free. There's no parole or probation officer and no GPS tracking device. The media portrayal of these criminals as *innocent* enables them to offend repeatedly because people aren't watching carefully. They don't think they have any reason to be suspicious of an *innocent* man.

Even more disturbing is the fact that some of the stories involve claims of money changing hands to create the false sense that a guilty man is actually innocent. As we saw with the Central Park Jogger case, there's nothing more persuasive, either in a real court or in the court of public opinion, than having someone else confess to the crime and claim that they acted alone. But a closer look at these "sole actor" confessions raises important questions about whether there might be more to these stories than meets the eye.

For one thing, isn't it at least a startling coincidence that in a few celebrated cases, the "real killer" (or rapist) who says he acted alone was "discovered" by the guy claiming to be wrongfully convicted? And isn't it interesting that the discovery was made at a time when both just *happened* to be spending time together behind bars in the same prison? Makes a person wonder. Did the guy claiming to be innocent offer the false confessor a reward of some sort - maybe a piece of the action when he wins millions in his "wrongful" conviction lawsuit? A guy in prison might be willing to take sole responsibility for a crime, even if it means he might do extra time behind bars, if it creates a substantial benefit for him, like a big pile of money that he can use for himself when he gets released, or give to his family on the outside. The most important question is, why isn't anyone investigating the money and/or influence trail in these cases?

In at least one case, there's an explicit claim of bribery. A guy named Alstory Simon said he was offered money to confess to murder and say that he acted alone. A man named Anthony Porter had already been convicted of the crime, and was on death row awaiting execution. Simon was offered money to say that Porter was not involved, and was completely innocent. This led to Porter's celebrated release from prison. Sometime later, Simon revealed that he had falsely confessed to committing the crime alone after receiving promises of lenient punishment as well as money and other rewards from book and movie deals about Porter's "rescue" from death row. The truth about all this remains murky, but at the very least, claims that a man would be offered money to falsely confess to murder (and that he would take it) are extremely disturbing

Thanks to people like Josh Marquis, the public is becoming appropriately skeptical. People are starting to understand that DNA rarely tells the whole story, even when it establishes the presence of an individual's body fluid at a certain location. Let's not forget that O. J. Simpson's lawyers (including Barry Sheck from the Innocence PrO.J.ect, hypocritically enough) claimed that when Ron Goldman's blood was discovered in Simpson's notorious white Bronco, it didn't necessarily prove Simpson's involvement in Goldman's murder. Laughable, I know, but the point is that if there *had* been an innocent explanation for that blood, the evidence wouldn't necessarily have proved Simpson's guilt.

The downside of all this DNA-lying is that the public ends up with the false impression that our criminal justice system desperately needs to make things better for accused criminals. And in truth, if the numbers of wrongly convicted innocent men were as high as the DNA lies suggest, it might be appropriate to spend time and resources fixing relevant systemic flaws. But because the number of innocent, wrongly convicted men is actually minuscule (something like .0001 percent) compared to the countless defendants who are wrongly acquitted and the millions of criminals who are guilty but never charged, it simply isn't reasonable to waste the public's money trying to make the system better for the bad guys.

The system will never be perfect. The very nature of jury trials means that imperfect human beings make decisions based on inherently imperfect sensory observations. Some cases are decided on the testimony of a single eyewitness, not because the system is unfair to criminals, but because that's all there is. Criminals try hard not to get caught. They tend not to commit crimes in front of many witnesses, and they do their best to avoid leaving behind a mountain of evidence because they don't want to go to prison. If the only evidence available to the prosecutor is the testimony of one eyewitness, and the jury believes that witness beyond a reasonable doubt, the accused should be found guilty, and we shouldn't feel bad about it.

DNA lies are not only distracting, they're also unfairly influencing the death penalty debate because abolitionists use claims about all the "innocent" men being released from prison to argue that capital punishment should be abolished altogether. Even though there's no proof that any innocent person has ever been executed, which is a pretty good track record, it's not right to make people change their minds about the death penalty by lying about the numbers of wrongfully convicted truly *innocent* men. Moral persuasion is one thing, and I'm personally opposed to the death penalty, but when the truth comes out about all the DNA lies, many people will return to a pro-death-penalty position with a vengeance.

DNA science holds great promise as a tool that can help identify the guilty and vindicate the innocent. It's a good thing that tests are becoming more readily available, less expensive, and can be done faster today than ever before. But the technology is no panacea, and we need to use this powerful scientific tool with our eyes wide open. It's too easy to be blinded by the gobbledygook of science and to accept claims that are difficult to rebut as being true because the topic is too complicated for most of us to understand.

We need more honest attention to claims of innocence in court, and we need more balance and truth-telling about these cases in the media, including much more coverage of cases where DNA testing confirms a man's guilt. For example, when a blind woman in Wisconsin, identified in the press only as Patty, was raped at knifepoint in 1997, she couldn't identify her attacker. Police not only doubted her credibility, they charged her with lying about the crime even though she'd gone to the hospital and submitted to a rape exam where DNA evidence was taken. In 2001, that DNA was matched to a convicted sex offender named Joseph Bong, and police, to their credit, apologized to Patty. They also paid her $35,000 to settle the lawsuit she filed against them. Thirty-five thousand dollars!? Many factually guilty but exonerated rapists get six figure settlements when they sue for their wrongful convictions. Patty got a token sum even though she suffered more than *any* guilty rapist who sat in prison for a crime he really *did* commit. Maybe even worse than the insultingly low settlement is the fact that the media paid almost no attention to the case. There were no front-page stories in major newspapers and no laudatory press conferences to feature the power of DNA to vindicate Patty and *prove* a man's guilt. Nothing at all, really, except for a couple of small stories in a local paper.

Until things get better for people like Patty, we can all take a stand by being openly skeptical of defense attorneys who make claims about DNA evidence and their clients' innocence. When the word "exonerated" is used in a news story, stop and ask yourself whether that means "actual innocence" or something else. For guidance on how to figure out the answer, check out the work of Dudley Sharp, whose articles are easy to find on the Internet and who has written a brilliant analysis of the misleading use of the words "exonerated" and "innocence" in death penalty cases.

Write letters to the editors of print media when reporters don't ask tough questions or don't seem to understand that "exonerated" does not mean "innocent." Hold your elected officials responsible by voting for candidates who will pass tough laws to prevent the waste of tax dollars on things like DNA tests that will violate a victim's privacy by revealing information about her consensual sex partners without any hope of proving a man's innocence, and lawsuits to compensate exonerated-but-factually-guilty criminals.

Finally, be a smart citizen when you get called for jury duty. Try hard not to be excessively impressed by evidence just because it's complicated or scientific or because a hired gun "expert" testifies in a way that makes the information sound important. As citizens beholden to the task of rendering fair judgments, we have to stand firm and confident in our ability to apply common sense and see the truth in every criminal trial – no matter how distracting the razzle-dazzle of technology.

THREE

Victory Through Intimidation

Here's more bad news: Victims and witnesses are literally walking away from criminal prosecutions because they've been harassed or threatened by the perpetrator, his buddies, or even his lawyer. I call it victory through intimidation. It happens in all kinds of cases, and in a variety of different ways.

Witnesses to gang violence are regularly threatened that they will be hurt or killed if they cooperate with police. Victims of rape and domestic violence are threatened with homelessness and the loss of their children if they don't "drop the charges," and even eyewitnesses to drunk driving cases are getting paid not to show up on the morning of trial.

Organized crime thugs have been killing off witnesses since the beginning of time (in the spirit of not leaving any loose ends behind). So witness intimidation isn't exactly new, but things are a lot worse today because of how bold and widespread these tactics are, and because so much intimidation occurs with the blessing (or at least the tacit cooperation) of the justice system itself.

In 2005, for example, gang members started wearing STOP SNITCHING T-shirts in and around the Boston courtrooms as a muted but malevolent reminder to witnesses that they would be in danger if they told the truth. No, this isn't just some sick manifestation of gang loyalty; it is a tactic specifically calculated to help the bad guys go free by making the witnesses afraid to speak. Period. Does anybody in the courtroom do anything about it? No. Why? Because they're afraid that the ACLU will file a lawsuit claiming that STOP SNITCHING T-shirts are protected by the First Amendment. But what about the fact that victims and witnesses have a Constitutional right to participate in judicial proceedings without intimidation? And what about the fact that the public has a right to everyone's testimony? When these values aren't protected because of fears that the ACLU will file a lawsuit, threats and intimidation tactics flourish.

Approximately 40 percent of murders in Massachusetts went unsolved in 2005. This is decent evidence that STOP SNITCHING strategies are working - and the justice system isn't.

Another common intimidation tactic occurs when defense attorneys exclude the victim's parents from the courtroom in child abuse cases. In the 2001 Massachusetts prosecution of Daniel Miller, who was being prosecuted for repeatedly sexually abusing a little boy, the child's parents were forced to sit outside the courtroom when the child took the stand because the defense attorney, Michael Bourbeau, told the court he intended to call the parents as witnesses.

The parents desperately wanted to be in the room to comfort their child with their presence as he confronted the monster charged with assaulting him. Bourbeau claimed, however, that the parents' testimony would be tainted by what they heard while the child was on the stand, so they were locked out.

As expected, the parents were never called to testify, but with his mom and dad out of the room, the child victim was all alone and terrified when he had to sit only a short distance from his attacker and tell a group of strangers about the terrible things that had happened to him.

Miller was acquitted. The tactic worked. The justice system didn't.

In another Massachusetts case, defense attorney Judith Lindahl sent subpoenas to various medical professionals who provided care to a minor rape victim before and after the crime. Huge files were turned over, filled with reams of irrelevant, sensitive information about the victim and her family.

Is it ever appropriate to violate a victim's privacy rights? Reasonable minds can disagree. In this case, however, the intrusion was outrageous because the victim was under the age of consent and there was DNA proof that the perpetrator had sexual contact with the victim. When the only issue in dispute is whether a sex act occurred, and it's been established by DNA evidence, there's no reason to violate an entire family's medical privacy rights.

Even if an argument could be made that the *victim's* treatment files should be released, it is unconscionable in the extreme for a judge to allow a defense attorney to violate the privacy rights of the *victim's parents* who had nothing to do with the crime.

An appeal to a Single Justice of the Massachusetts Supreme Judicial Court later that year was unavailing. The judge assigned to the case, Martha Sosman (who has since passed away), expressed little concern for the gratuitous damage to the privacy rights of the victim and her parents. In fact, Justice Sosman was already on record as believing that the law should permit virtually automatic access to the private records of all rape victims. It was no surprise then when, in my case, she expressed no concern for the privacy rights of the victim or her parents. Justice Sosman wanted to use her position as an appellate judge to change the law to fit her ideology. In my opinion, this activist agenda interfered with Sosman's capacity to be a fair jurist.

The victim and her family ultimately walked away from the case. They couldn't take it anymore and the charges were dismissed. Thanks to Justice Sosman, an accused rapist walked free.

In a similar case, the 2003 criminal rape prosecution of a defendant named Manuel Valverde, defense attorney Paul Rudof insisted on the full disclosure of a rape victim's crisis counseling file, while openly conceding that he had no idea what was in there, why he needed it, or how violating the victim's Constitutional rights was necessary to protect the defendant's rights. Even worse was the way Rudof found out that the victim had received crisis counseling after the rape. His private investigator, paid for by public tax dollars, repeatedly contacted and harassed the victim's grandmother (her legal guardian at the time) and pestered her with probing questions about personal issues. Like what? Well, like whether the victim had ever been abused as a child, and whether the grandmother herself had ever been charged with a crime or received assistance from social services.

The grandmother resisted the investigator's demands initially, but on one occasion, when the grandmother was sick in bed, the investigator showed up again to ask questions. She finally relented and told the investigator that the victim sought counseling after the rape at a local crisis center. The defense wasted no time sending a subpoena for the file.

The crisis center resisted the subpoena and told the judge about the victim's grandmother being harassed by the defense. They explained that the grandmother started crying when she learned that her statement to the investigator was helping the defense intimidate her granddaughter.

Rather than punishing the defense, the judge, a former public defender, threatened the center with contempt and a fine of $500 per day unless they turned over the file.

The crisis center couldn't afford the electric bill much less a $500 fine for a single day, so I filed an emergency motion with the appellate court to put a stop to the fine and allow us to appeal the contempt judgment. The media was covering the case, thankfully, and the public was outraged that a judge not only would order disclosure of a confidential file without cause, but also punish an impoverished crisis center with a $500 per day fine.

With the help of a nonprofit organization called "Stop Family Violence," I started a petition drive and got 500 people to agree to spend one night in jail, each, in lieu of the $500 fine. We eventually got thousands of people to sign on, but as soon as we had five hundred names, I attached the list of protestors to my appellate brief and argued that it was important for the court to understand how strongly the public felt about protecting medical privacy rights for innocent crime victims. It should matter to the court, I argued, that complete strangers were willing to go to jail to stop an injustice.

It worked for a while. We won an initial stay of the fine, and it helped that the *New York Times* covered the case. But when the public protest died down months later, the court ruled against us. This was not unexpected because several (but not all) appellate judges in Massachusetts just don't like it when victims stand up for their rights. But it is an important lesson in the value of public protest. When people make much noise about injustice, judges pay attention.

Some defense attorneys complain that public protests in support of victims' rights are a form of vigilantism, and that victims have no business objecting when defense attorneys demand the release of a victim's confidential files. They claim the accused has a "Constitutional right to conduct fishing expeditions." This is silly, of course, because Constitutional rights apply only to files in the custody of the defendant's opponent, the prosecutor. The defense attorney can snoop around in the *prosecutor's* file all he wants, but not the *victim's* medical file. Fishing expeditions are always wrong not only because there is no Constitutional legal relationship between the accused and the victim, but also because crime victims should never be forced to choose between healing and justice.

Defense attorneys say it's important to inspect a victim's medical files because "you never know" what might be in there. But they could say that about every medical file of every witness in every case. Imagine the outrage if Bernie Madoff's attorney said he had a "Constitutional right" to read through the medical files of each of Madoff's victims. Or let's say you're a guy in line at a bank, and you see a man commit an armed robbery. You give a statement to police and later you tell your wife about what happened, and she writes about it in her diary. Should the robber be allowed to force your wife to give him her diary so he can read through the whole thing, on the theory that "you never know" what might be in there? What if instead of telling your spouse, you tell your priest or your lawyer? Should the priest be forced to testify about what you said? Should the lawyer's files be sent to the defense so they can conduct a fishing expedition under the "you never know" rule? Of course not.

Judges know there's no such thing as a "Constitutional right" to demand access to a victim's grocery receipts, much less confidential files. But many judges were once defense lawyers and when they put on their robes, they don't care about the law. They let defense attorneys run roughshod over the privacy rights of victims because that's what *they* wanted to do when they were practicing law.

To a defense attorney, being allowed access to a victim's confidential file is a victory. To me, it's a disgrace. It's why I started fighting for victims in the first place.

Back in 1992, I generated my first test case in an attempt to change the law so that victims' privacy rights would have better legal protections. As a prosecutor between 1987 and 1992, I had seen too many victims walk away from cases after they were told that the perpetrator was getting copies of their confidential records.

To set up a good test case, I advised a rape crisis center to refuse to obey the next subpoena for a victim's file. As predicted, the judge held the center in contempt, which enabled us to file an appeal. The judge ruled that we had a good faith objection to the subpoena, so she didn't impose any sanctions, and she put a hold on the criminal trial until our appeal was done.

The public was on our side, and it soon became clear that we were going to win our appeal and change the law, but before the appellate court had a chance to rule, the strangest thing happened - the defense lawyer, Catherine Byrne, had her client plead guilty and go to prison for eight to ten years. Then she demanded that my appeal be dismissed as moot.

Here's what's interesting about this. Byrne's client was free on very low bail at the time. He would have stayed out of jail for at least another year while our appeal was being decided. Yet Byrne had the guy give up his freedom and go to prison *for eight to ten years* so that she could stop us from changing the law. So much for Byrne's concern for her client's liberty and due process rights. She initially said her client couldn't get a fair trial unless he had a chance to review the victim's counseling file. But when we were on the verge of winning, she did a 180, no longer cared about the file, and sent the guy to prison, *not* because she had an epiphany about his guilt but to stop us from winning a precedent-setting decision. Unbelievable!

I considered filing an ethical complaint against Byrne because as much as I didn't give a damn about the rapist, the guy was entitled to a fair trial, and his lawyer wasn't doing her job. To this day, I don't think Byrne's client has a clue why he was advised to plead guilty.

The good news is, Byrne's strategy ultimately failed. I found an obscure case that said my appeal was not moot because the "stigma of contempt" deserves appellate attention even when the underlying case is resolved. My appeal was allowed to proceed, and we won a major decision that changed the law and improved legal protections for all victims' private files.

That wasn't the only time I've seen a defense attorney try to derail an appeal to prevent an appellate court from improving the law on behalf of victims. Defense lawyers have far too much control over appeals in criminal cases, and the evolution of criminal law. They often head up key criminal justice committees in state legislatures, and they control powerful rule-making boards where decisions are made that affect criminal justice policy. The defense bar also has much greater access to appellate courts compared to prosecutors and victims, and they can cherry-pick the issues they bring to appeal, which significantly shapes the evolution of criminal law doctrines.

It's worse in some states, like Massachusetts, where prosecutors rarely pursue their own appeals because it's simply too expensive. It's actually doubly expensive compared to the cost imposed on public defenders' budgets because, win or lose, when prosecutors appeal, they are forced to pay not only their own costs, but also the costs of the defense. In many cases, we're talking about *your* tax dollars creating a financial disincentive for prosecutors to file appeals and correct injustices.

Appellate courts don't love it when prosecutors file appeals, but they're downright hostile when a victim does. But I do it all the time, and I win most of my cases, though when I'm right, courts are reluctant to say so because they don't want to encourage other lawyers to do what I do. In fact, in one of my first and hardest fought cases, the appellate court that ruled in my favor announced its decision to change the law, exactly as I had requested, *in someone else's case*!

I know what I think of that. What do you think of that?

For my part, I didn't give a damn about the lost glory. What mattered was changing the law, not getting credit for the win. (The press figured it out, so I got some credit.) But by issuing the ruling in someone else's case (where the lawyers never even addressed the issue, much less *asked* the court to change the law) the court sent a strong message to me that I should *not* make a career out of challenging the system and changing the law to help crime victims.

In the wake of that moment, I knew I had to make an important decision. Should I continue with the type of work that was so important to victims but annoying to the system, or should I move on to the "real world" of lawyering and avoid controversy?

I chose to continue the fight for victims, and after more than twenty years, it's clear I made the right decision. I've changed the law many times, all over the country, and won many important victories for individual victims, but more needs to be done.

First, we need to send a zero-tolerance message to the types of wayward defense attorneys who engage in unethical tactics like harassing victims' grandmothers. Such lawyers should be punished with mandatory economic and licensing sanctions for the first offense, and worse, if they don't get the message the first time.

We also need, in every state, an entity where victims can go to report defense attorney misconduct. The best model today, combining oversight and accountability, is the Alaska Office on Victims' Rights (AOVR). The AOVR functions something like an inspector general's office. When a victim's rights are violated, an investigator can issue subpoenas and interrogate individuals to determine whether punishment is appropriate. For example, under Alaska law, all defense interviews with victims must be recorded, and victims must be advised of their right not to answer questions. If this is not done, a victim can file a complaint with the AOVR. Attorneys who engage in improper tactics can then be identified in a public report published annually by the AOVR. It's not much of a stick as sanctions go, but in conjunction with the possibility of fines and licensing sanctions, it's substantially better than what most states have now, which is nothing.

Another important remedy, as I mentioned in chapter one, involves regular auditing of public defenders' budgets to make sure the system isn't wasting tax money on overpayments to lawyers and private investigators who are using public dollars to intimidate crime victims and their families.

We also need more legal support for victims who refuse to comply with unjust subpoenas and court orders. By allowing more third-party objections in court, and appeals when those objections are unsuccessful, victims can hold the system accountable while bringing public awareness to the kinds of defense tactics that cause needless harm to innocent victims and undermine respect for the rule of law.

Finally, victims need to start filing lawsuits against unethical defense attorneys and defense investigators. I don't say this lightly, and it shouldn't be done often. But it can work wonders. When I did it, not only did the lawyer I sued stop sending unlawful subpoenas to victims and their doctors, but when other attorneys found out that I'd successfully sued a defense lawyer for these practices, they stopped using unfair tactics against crime victims, too. Yes, lawsuits can be abused, but a well-chosen and vigorously pursued claim against a ruthless defense lawyer can serve as a highly effective kind of quality-control device - one that inspires better behavior from attorneys who wouldn't otherwise give a damn about the rules.

FOUR

Race Baiting

When the name of the game is defense at any cost, truth doesn't matter - nor does exploiting bigotry and prejudice, even when the collateral damage to our social fabric is enormous.

For certain types of defense attorneys, there are no limits. Playing the race or gender card is perfectly acceptable because, as they see it, justice itself is irrelevant during a criminal trial. Forget truth and fairness; winning is the only goal. It's about bragging rights at the local pub, where defense lawyers one-up each other with tales of the latest vile trick they've used to get a guilty criminal off scot-free.

Think I'm exaggerating? I'm not. O. J. Simpson is a free man today because his lawyers played the defense-at-any-cost game by using the race card in a massive, relentless way, convincing the jurors that the loathsome Simpson was on trial for murder only because a group of racist government officials had it in for Simpson. Forget the mountain of evidence, when the defense proved that Mark Fuhrman, the lead detective on the case, had used the N-word, the case was over.

Make no mistake about it: Defense attorneys will gladly whip the public and jurors into a frenzy over any hot-button social issue if it might divert attention away from the real evidence and help even the most dangerous criminal walk free.

Kobe Bryant's lawyer, Pamela Mackey, did it during Bryant's rape trial when she held forth in open court in January 2004 that "there is a lot of history about black men being falsely accused of this crime by white women." Note that Mackey played two cards at once - race and gender - a neat trick that gets twice the bang for half the buck because many people don't even notice the gender card.

Gender bias is so pervasive and so passively accepted in rape cases, that using sexism against the victim isn't even seen as playing a card, much less an offensive, bigoted one. So mixing race and gender bias to claim that white women have a history of falsely accusing black men of rape worked effectively to ignite a big fire of public rage against the victim.

Forget that research shows almost all rapes occur between people of the same race; that the false-allegation rate is minuscule (people are far more likely to falsely report their own death for insurance fraud purposes); and that, while some women and men do make false accusations of rape, there is no evidence they're made disproportionately by white women against black men. For some lawyers, it doesn't matter that the tactic perpetuates harmful myths that are destructive to society.

No matter how much we care about the rights of the accused, no single man's freedom is worth the perpetuation of racism. But Kobe Bryant's and O. J. Simpson's lawyers simply didn't care. Simpson's lawyers knew that if the jury thought the lead detective on the case was racist, the real evidence wouldn't matter. Likewise, Kobe Bryant's lawyers knew that invoking images of black men being lynched in the antebellum South would have the public talking more about slavery than rape.

As we all saw firsthand, race baiting was so effective in Simpson's case, it dragged jurors' attention away from unassailable evidence of guilt, proving the theory that the more powerful the prosecution's case, the bigger the distraction has to be, and the prosecution's case against Simpson was damn strong.

No judge in his or her right mind should permit the strategic exploitation of prejudice as a trial strategy. Judge Ruckreigle, in Bryant's case, should have held Mackey in contempt for making such an idiotic and incendiary statement, and Judge Lance Ito should have forbidden the defense to ask *any* witness whether they've ever used the N-word. But Judge Ito caved to the outside pressure instead, and turned a murder trial into a racism-tinged theatre of vengeance and manipulation.

What kind of pressure am I talking about? Well, let's not forget that there were angry crowds outside the courthouse almost every day throughout Simpson's trial. Why were they there? In part, because the case happened so soon after the Rodney King case, which rightly upset many people in this country. The defense team certainly understood the moment they were dealing with, but Judge Ito's job was to rise above the climate, not indulge it, and incite even more anger.

Whatever the injustices in the Rodney King case, a double murderer should not have walked away scot-free as a quid pro quo to make up for what happened to Mr. King. The defense lawyers who thought it was appropriate to use an injustice against one black man to provoke even more racism should apologize to all Americans, especially racial minorities.

My question is: How exactly do we get the F. Lee Baileys of the world, who are willing to exploit racism to win criminal trials, to pay back society for the harm they cause to race relations for an entire nation? And how do we stop another generation of junior F. Lee Baileys from doing the same thing in the future?

It won't be easy, in part because there are so many Bailey-types out there who will stop at nothing to win. Take, for example, defense attorney Robert George, who adopted pretty much the same strategy in the Cape Cod trial of a black man named Christopher McCowen. McCowen was prosecuted for the murder of socialite, Christa Worthington, who was stabbed to death in her home in the remote oceanside town of Truro, Massachusetts. Police solved the crime when they identified the DNA found in Worthington's genital area as belonging to McCowen, who was Worthington's garbage man. McCowen all but confessed to the crime, telling police he had sex with her and beat her but didn't kill her. He then claimed that a friend of his stabbed the victim. Unfortunately for McCowen, his intended fall guy had a solid alibi. When McCowen was told that his friend couldn't possibly have done it, he replied that he realized he alone would likely be held accountable.

Attorney George argued to the jury that because his client is black, police and prosecutors were racist for arresting his client. He claimed that racism had led the police to arrest his client because they simply couldn't accept the reality of a white socialite having consensual sex with a black garbage man. Of course, George conveniently left out the fact that his client had more or less confessed to the heinous crime. But my point is that there's nothing racist about police concluding the killer was the guy who admitted to beating the victim and whose DNA just happened to be found in her body. That the guy was black had nothing to do with the evidence that sealed his fate.

But that didn't stop Attorney George. (He was sent to federal prison for committing his own crimes in 2012.) After falsely accusing the police of racism, he engaged in his own pernicious brand of racism and sexism by telling the jury that they should believe Worthington had consensual sex with McCowen because she had a history of engaging in sex acts with social undesirables. It's an astonishing statement when you think about it. After complaining that McCowen was only in trouble because the cops were racist, George himself labeled his client a social undesirable because he was . . . poor? A garbage man? Black?

The silence from antiracism activists was deafening. I, and precious few others, complained publicly about George's race-baiting strategy, but a number of defense attorneys argued that George had a right to exploit social prejudice to help his client win, whether it was legitimately an issue in the case or not.

The system badly needs an overhaul to deal with the exploitation of bigotry as a trial tactic. One solution is what is known in California as the snitch-rule. The idea grew out of public disgust with the O. J. Simpson verdict. It simply requires jurors to rat out other jurors who refuse to deliberate honestly, or who render decisions based on improper criteria. In other words, a juror who says, "I'm voting 'not guilty' because I want to cut the defendant some slack as a black man" would be removed from jury service. So would the juror who declares, "I'm voting 'guilty' because the defendant is a black man." These are both highly improper statements and any juror who says such a thing should be dismissed. But defense attorneys argue that only the jurors who vote "guilty" based on racism should be excluded. Those who would acquit a man based on skin color should be celebrated – as if racism is acceptable so long as it leads to the unwarranted release of a dangerous murderer or rapist.

Prosecutors need to find a way to challenge unjust acquittals when the result is directly caused by discrimination against a particular social class. This might require a Constitutional amendment to address double jeopardy concerns, which of course would take a long time and much effort, but someone needs to get the ball rolling before we embarrass ourselves again on the world stage with another O. J. fiasco.

It would help, in the meantime, if we could perform better screening of jurors for all types of serious biases, not just those that might disadvantage the accused. In 2005, the jurors in the Michael Jackson case were screened for race prejudice, which, of course, is a good thing, but they were also screened to determine whether they or anyone close to them had ever been abused as a child. This was supposed to ensure the jurors wouldn't be too sympathetic to the victim, but is the question really fair? Many people are close to someone who was abused as a child, but this doesn't make them incompetent to serve as jurors in child-abuse cases. In fact, it probably makes them particularly good jurors because they have more familiarity with the subject matter, and can better assess the evidence presented.

While the potentially sympathetic jurors were being screened out in Jackson's case, nobody was asking a single question of the jurors to determine whether they, or anyone close to them, had ever sexually abused a child, or even whether any of them were members of the North American Man/Boy Love Association (NAMBLA), which believes that sex between adults and children should be legal. We have no idea whether the jurors who voted to acquit Jackson belonged to NAMBLA at the time because nobody asked.

We also need women defense lawyers to stop exploiting their gender to help win rape cases. In chapter three, I told you about the way defense lawyers violate victims' privacy rights by demanding access to privileged counseling files. It's bad enough that this ugly tactic is disproportionately used to intimidate female rape victims, it's downright creepy when female defense lawyers use their gender to make the tactic seem legitimate.

When I was fighting to change the law in Massachusetts to better protect victims' privacy rights, efforts to derail my work were supported by self-described "women's rights" advocates. In one of those cases, I filed an appeal to overturn the infamous *Stockhammer* case, where the court ruled that defense attorneys should be given automatic and unfettered access to victims' privileged medical records, without any showing of need, and without having a judge first conduct a private review of the file to see whether it contained any important evidence.

The ruling was both preposterous and unconstitutional, and when it became apparent that my appeal would probably be successful, defense lawyers got nervous. One of them, a "feminist" criminal attorney named Nancy Gertner, got especially nervous because she was the lawyer who originally won the *Stockhammer* case, and she wanted to preserve her victory.

Unbeknownst to me, Gertner was, then, serving on a board of the NOW Legal Defense and Education Fund, a women's rights organization that I had already contacted about writing a brief in support of my position. Without my knowledge, Gertner offered to write NOW's brief, and I did not see what she wrote until the morning of oral argument.

I was stunned to read that instead of supporting my side, as NOW had promised they would, Gertner's brief argued that the *Stockhammer* ruling should be upheld and that there should be no privacy protections for victims' privileged counseling files. Gertner insisted that accused rapists should have automatic access to victims' private files without establishing a need for the information, and without having the files first submitted to the judge for a private or *in-camera* review.

During this time, a friend of Gertner's and self-described "feminist" advocate for rape victims, Susan Estrich, penned an opinion piece for a national news magazine making the same arguments as Gertner. As the old saying goes, "With friends [or women's rights advocates] like these, who needs enemies?"

It's one thing for a criminal lawyer to oppose victims' privacy rights, but a women's rights group the magnitude of NOW Legal Defense had no business undermining the ability of victims to obtain confidential treatment in the aftermath of rape. Their brief was a manipulative, dishonest and dangerous document that threatened to hurt our chances of overturning the *Stockhammer* ruling, not because it was persuasive or well-written, but because it had been submitted on behalf of a leading women's rights organization. If a group like NOW didn't care about protecting privacy rights for rape victims, the court might well assume (wrongly) that all women's groups felt the same way.

I was outraged by Gertner's covert tactics and insulted by her arguments. I asked other women's groups around the country to join me in signing a letter demanding that NOW immediately withdraw the brief and have it removed from the court's file.

When Gertner learned what I was doing, she asked me to lunch to see whether I would agree to a compromise. Rather than withdrawing her brief, she offered to modify it by arguing that the defense should have to make a showing of need before a victim's files could be released. She insisted, however, that there should be no private screening by the judge and that if enough of a showing is made, the files should be sent directly to the defense.

I refused her offers and told her to pull the brief immediately, in its entirety. A few days later, Gertner sent a letter to the Supreme Judicial Court informing them that her brief was no longer authorized by NOW Legal Defense and should be withdrawn.

Three months later, we won a resounding victory and Gertner's *Stockhammer* ruling was overturned.

When *Lawyers' Weekly* ran a story on the landmark decision, the editors noted that Nancy Gertner was listed as one of the lawyers who submitted a brief in the case. But when the final official decision was published about a month later, Gertner's and NOW's names were missing. *Lawyers' Weekly* reporters tried to investigate why Gertner's name had been removed, and they even wrote a follow-up piece entitled "The Nancy Withdrew Mystery," speculating that Gertner had pulled the brief because she was, by then, being considered for a federal judgeship in Massachusetts.

I didn't tell anyone the truth because I thought Gertner would make a good federal judge on issues like equal pay for women. I also wanted her out of the business of messing up my cases. Years later, Gertner retired from the federal bench and started teaching. I hope her students listen very carefully, and skeptically, when she talks about women's rights and the legal system's unfair treatment of rape victims. And who knows, maybe Gertner will have an epiphany in her old age, and she'll start teaching law students about why exploiting sexism in the name of justice is dangerous to democracy and should be forbidden in legal proceedings, no matter which side it helps or hurts.

Allowing any prejudice to produce unfair verdicts *in the name of justice* gives value to all bigotry, and so long as prejudice has strategic value in a court of law, discrimination will flourish in the real world.

Think of all the role models in our society, the teachers, spiritual leaders, business people, and politicians who work hard every day to fight discrimination in society. Are we being fair to them? Are we honoring their noble work when we let lawyers fan the flames of prejudice for sport?

I don't think so.

F I V E

Winning Through Payoffs and Extortion

It's certainly not news that rich criminals get better treatment than poor ones. It's just one of those realities that we can talk about and fight against but never quite eliminate. I can accept that life is generally easier for people with a lot of money.

But for our purposes in this chapter, we have to take it to another level. Benefiting from wealth is one thing; corrupting justice with payoffs and extortion is a whole other kettle of fish. Yes, money can and does buy the best lawyer. And that's fine, but money shouldn't be able to buy witnesses or the outright dismissal of criminal charges.

Yet payoffs and extortion seem commonplace in today's criminal justice system. Every time you turn around, there's another story about a key witness in a criminal case simply not showing up for trial. All too often, you hear that a critical piece of evidence went missing or has somehow become tainted, but there's no explanation or investigation to determine whether some form of corruption is afoot.

So what's the message? I guess if you're contemplating committing a crime, you should get rich first.

I know this sounds cynical, and maybe you're not even surprised. After all, phrases like "money walks" and "rich man's justice" have been around for a long time. But, at least, we used to complain about it. We used to think it was wrong and that someone should do something about it.

I'm not sure why we stopped caring, but I think it started around the time Michael Jackson bought his way out of a criminal prosecution in 1993. How much did Jackson have to spend to thwart justice back then? The answer, according to Michael's father, Joe Jackson, is $22 million. Joe told CNN's Piers Morgan in January 2013 that trying to keep the payoff a secret caused the superstar much grief. Indeed.

$22 million bucks is a whopper of a payoff, which suggests that the evidence against Jackson was of blockbuster quality, and as we later found out, the clincher was reportedly testimony from the child victim detailing unusual markings on Jackson's genitals, something about which a child who hadn't been molested would have no way of knowing. When cops confirmed that the child was right about the markings, the cash started flowing.

Lady Justice is supposed to be blind. In Michael Jackson's case, she was more like a blind, deaf, and dumb pimp - facilitating a walk for Jackson when he should have been locked up for a long, long time. The guy was accused of child rape, after all. (Yes, it was rape. The allegations involved penile/oral penetration.) But after the payoff, the victim conveniently changed his tune from that of a cooperating witness to a victim who refused to testify.

Paying a victim for silence should be prosecuted as obstruction of justice, and the lawyers who brokered the deal, Johnny Cochran for Jackson and Larry Feldman for the victim, should have been treated as criminals, pure and simple.

Emboldened by his payoff "victory," Jackson flaunted his ability to molest kids with impunity by appearing in public with little boys in pajamas, writing a song taunting the frustrated prosecutor, and eventually boasting on international television that he often sleeps in his bed with little boys. Sometimes when I hear these stories, I picture the framers of our Constitution cringing at the idea of Michael Jackson thumbing his fake nose at the justice system with one hand while grabbing the rear end of a little boy with the other. And I'm certain they would have torn the Constitution up and started all over if they knew that O. J. Simpson would one day use the First and Fifth Amendments to make a small fortune on his book, *If I Did It*, where he hypothetically confessed to the murders of Ron Goldman and Nicole Brown.

Though the book was eventually pulled from bookstores, Simpson managed to pocket a reported six-figure sum in advance because the publisher saw value in revealing how and why Simpson slaughtered two innocent people. The most horrible part of this ugliness is that the value of Simpson's musings was created, in part, by our precious Fifth Amendment.

The Fifth Amendment is a key Constitutional freedom that allows citizens to remain silent during police interrogations because forcing an individual to become a witness against himself is anathema to the ideals of a free society. But while the Fifth Amendment protects silence, it nowhere states that the criminal can then trade on the value of that silence by selling the truth in a book or movie about the crime.

Can you see how sick and perverted this is? We have a Constitution that allows murderers to keep secrets about their crimes - to protect liberty for all of us - but nothing prevents them from turning the value of that secret into profit, and literally exploiting the sacred nature of an essential freedom by using it as a pawn in a seedy business deal. Sure, people were outraged, and the book was never widely released, but because Simpson was paid a ton of money up front, the damage to the Constitution was done.

Shame on all the brokers who got a piece of the action by jerking a First Amendment knee and defending themselves by saying Simpson had the Constitutional "right" to do it. The fact that he *could* do it didn't mean they had to help make it happen.

Before the next killer tries the same trick, I propose that we pass a law requiring that, at the very least, all proceeds from such books or movies be paid to the victims or their families. And, while we're at it, let's make it a little bit harder for an acquitted wife-killer who seeks to profit from the sale of his story to win custody of his children. Kids should never be forced to live with their mother's killer, but can't we at least protect them from being forced to live with a guy who's selling books about how he slit mommy's throat?

Loving parents, especially protective mothers, too often lose custody of their children to dangerous men for far less serious transgressions. A guy like Simpson should never have been allowed the privilege of raising anyone's children, much less the children *of the woman he murdered*! And when the jerk decided to *sell* rather than *tell* the truth, someone from our legal system should have sent an apology letter to his kids for everything it did that emboldened Simpson to write the book.

Maybe Simpson took a lesson from Michael Jackson, who paid cash for a victim's silence, then flaunted the fact that he'd gotten away with a serious crime by continuing to engage in inappropriate activity with little boys. Why wouldn't a guy like Simpson think he could mock the legal system, too, by telling the truth in the name of profit after refusing to tell the truth in the name of justice?

Even the good guys didn't complain when Jackson bought his way out of prosecution in the early 1990s. Everyone on all sides of the payoff, including the victim and his family, should hang their heads in shame and should apologize to society for the ripple effect that followed, including our newfound tolerance for all forms of corruption. The prosecutor, Tom Sneddon, who was said to be furious about the Jackson payoff, bears some of the blame, too. He could have sent the victim a subpoena and forced him to testify, holding him in jail if necessary until he told the truth.

Sneddon should have insisted that the victim take the stand, if only to show that he doesn't tolerate corruption. Key witnesses to bank robberies aren't allowed to take payoffs in exchange for not testifying. Prosecutors make them take the stand because bank robbery is a serious crime. Isn't the rape of a child a serious crime, too?

We can't afford to have an exception in the law that lets certain types of witnesses take payoffs, while others have to cooperate. Justice is not a swap meet. I'll say it again. Justice has to be better than capitalism if we want people to respect the rule of law and treat each other with civility.

Defense attorneys are wrong when they say payoffs are O.K. because "at least the victim gets something for her suffering." Victims should participate in the criminal justice system, and *then* sue the perpetrator for money if they want. I represent victims in both types of cases all the time, and I don't need my clients to walk away from the criminal case to get them a ton of cash in the civil case.

I also don't want my client to give the government a pass for not doing its job by allowing rich criminals to avoid punishment while the poor, disproportionately minority men, rot in jail.

It's not only criminal lawyers who need to get this straight. Civil plaintiff lawyers deserve some of the blame because they engage in the flip side of payoffs when they extort extra money to take advantage of the fact that a defendant wants to keep ugly information out of the public arena. What do I mean by this? When someone wealthy or important commits the kind of crime that could also form the basis for a civil lawsuit, but the civil case isn't worth much money because, for example, the victim endured only minor injuries, the plaintiff's lawyer can demand more than what the civil case is worth as a price for not reporting the crime to cops, or not cooperating with prosecutors. This is not good lawyering. It is extortion. It is unethical. And, it happens all the time.

Consider the lawyers who demanded more than $2 million from President Bill Clinton to settle Paula Jones's claim that he sexually harassed her by pulling his pants down. Maybe it was a valid claim. Who knows? But two million bucks? How scary is a penis? The case was worth $100,000 on its best day; the rest was pure extortion.

To fix this craziness, we need new laws that expressly forbid victims to have any control over whether charges are "dropped" after they're initiated by the government.

I'm not saying the victim's feelings are irrelevant, or that testifying is the only thing that matters. But dismissing serious criminal charges because the victim would rather have money is not only wrong, it also releases dangerous criminals to our communities, empowered to believe they are untouchable and can commit crimes with impunity.

We need new laws that require full public disclosure of the financial records of victims, witnesses, and defendants whenever evidence of corruption is evident. If there's any hint of a payoff, the public has a right and a need to know about it so that everyone involved can be held accountable.

Finally, we need laws that forbid the filing of civil lawsuits by victims until the related criminal case has ended, alongside other laws that put the statute of limitations on hold so that the victim's right to sue doesn't expire while the criminal case is slogging along. These things will prevent problems like what occurred in the Kobe Bryant case where the dismissal of the criminal case just happened to coincide with the settlement of a related civil lawsuit, which just happened to occur on the eve of the criminal trial. The civil case looked like a sham from the get-go - a convenient excuse and seemingly legitimate vehicle through which a payoff could ultimately be made.

The public should have been more suspicious, and people should have been up in arms because they shelled out a small fortune getting the criminal case ready for trial, only to have the readiness of the case used as leverage to jack up the value of the victim's civil suit. (The civil case has far more "value" if the plaintiff's lawyer holds out until the eve of trial.) The victim got a windfall, Bryant walked free and the public got screwed. The victim and Bryant should *at least* repay the people of Colorado the costs associated with investigating and preparing the case for prosecution.

We won't ever flush the influence of money out of the system. But we can stop lawyers from posting virtual JUSTICE FOR SALE signs and prevent the spread of infectious disrespect for the law that comes with even passive acceptance of outright corruption.

S I X

Using Delay Strategically

Almost everyone has heard of the "right to a speedy trial." It was built into our legal system (in the Sixth and Fourteenth Amendments to the Constitution) by wise men who understood the dangers of having government officials seize people off the street, lock them up, and never quite get around to bringing them to trial. Freedom for all of us is better protected by enforcement of the right to a speedy (and public) trial.

Innocent people, in particular, benefit tremendously when a criminal case moves along swiftly. They get their freedom (and their lives) back faster, minimize legal expenses, and have their good names restored as quickly as possible.

But speedy trials are rarely demanded by accused criminals because almost all of them are guilty of something, and they sure don't want to rush their personal Judgment Day. This is why the typical defendant asks not for a speedy trial but, instead, for the slowest damn trial he can possibly hold out for.

When cases get delayed, guilty criminals benefit because witnesses die and move away. Memories fade, emotions subside, and evidence gets lost. As the old saying goes, "A good defense, like a good wine, gets better with age."

Let's look at a particularly odiferous case in point. Hollywood actor Robert Blake was acquitted in the 2001 murder of his wife after the case dragged on for years. Blake had hired and fired four different defense lawyers. One lawyer after another quit or was fired, virtually on the eve of each trial date. His first two lawyers claimed they resigned after Blake did media interviews against their advice. His third lawyer, Thomas Mesereau, stepped down right before trial was to begin, citing "irreconcilable differences."

Maybe Mesereau was telling the truth, but all too often when a lawyer cites "irreconcilable differences," it means either that the defendant refused to pay his legal fees or that the criminal and his lawyer are strategically trying to force the court to grant a delay in the trial. Most judges will give a lawyer newly assigned to a case a lot of time to prepare, even if they suspect the change in attorneys is a delay tactic. They worry that not allowing a delay could become an issue on appeal, so they indulge all sorts of tricks because it's efficient.

Efficiency was no excuse for so many delays in Blake's case. Judge Darlene Schempp should have had the guts to tell Blake to knock it off after the first lawyer was bumped. She should have said, "You're going to trial with or without a lawyer, and if you pull this stunt again, I'll put you in jail for contempt." Judge Schempp should have admonished Blake that there's no such thing as a Constitutional right to keep firing lawyers until all the witnesses drop dead. But judges with backbone are hard to find these days, especially in high-profile cases.

Delay tactics have been around for a very long time, but the boldness of this sick strategy seems to be spreading and some of the excuses are so lame it's a wonder the whole courtroom doesn't burst out laughing. They're like the old "dog ate my homework" line, except that the excuses are usually even less believable, and the stakes are far higher.

Judges rarely raise a skeptical eyebrow, much less punish defense attorneys for causing needless delays. I remember one lawyer, back when I was a prosecutor, who had a horrible reputation for causing delays in his cases. People in the courthouse used to joke about how his grandmother must have been a cat because he delayed his clients' trials to go to her funeral at least nine times. Funny enough, until you start to think about the devastating affect of these delays on victims who can't begin to get on with their lives until the criminal case is over.

I recall vividly the day when a rape victim client said to me, after her trial had been delayed for a second time, "If the defense attorney gets to drag this out one more time, I won't be able to handle it." She strongly implied that she might hurt herself. She had been under tremendous stress preparing for the trial, revisiting the terrible memories again, thinking hard about the night a stranger broke into her dorm room and attacked her repeatedly at knifepoint. She was ready for trial the first time, nerves steeled and misgivings squelched, mentally prepared to face the man who brutalized her, only to have the judge send everyone home after Boston defense attorney Mary Ames got her wish to put the case on hold.

Ames acted as though demanding a delay in the trial was no more important than rescheduling a dental appointment. The defendant caught a break while the victim literally fell over in physical pain. Ames is now a judge, which doesn't bode well for victims in her courtroom who hope their cases will be resolved promptly.

Delays also cost taxpayers a lot of money. Defense attorneys driven by ideology know that by making prosecutions more expensive, fewer cases can be pursued. "It's good for freedom," say the militant anti-law enforcement ideologues who believe that if they force the court system to waste time and money, they are somehow protecting civil liberties by preventing prosecutors from having enough resources to take on more cases.

We really could be doing a much better job prosecuting far more criminals if someone put a stop to strategic delay tactics. Tying the government's hands by jacking up the cost of prosecution doesn't protect freedom for anyone. It hurts civil liberties because by squeezing the justice system's budget, people who are trying their best to respect the Constitutional rights of criminals are forced to cut corners, which means the due process rights of all accused criminals suffer.

If defense attorneys really cared about freedom, they would do everything in their power to expedite trials to ensure that the system has the capacity to allow delays for those defendants who really need the extra time to prepare for and receive a fair trial. When the Robert Blakes of the world drag their cases out for no good reason, defendants who can't afford to keep hiring and firing lawyers get shortchanged. It's simple economics. People like Blake demand unfair advantages, and basic fairness for all accused criminals takes a hit.

This kind of greedy bog-down-the-system tactic was readily apparent in a recent case out of Pennsylvania, where a man was convicted of multiple sex crimes after what the court described as a "savage" assault. Evidence was "overwhelming," according to the court, and it was proved beyond all doubt that the perpetrator brutally raped an unconscious seventeen-year-old girl with a light bulb, a shot glass, and a hanger - in front of witnesses. After the conviction, the rapist's lawyer filed a massive appeal, raising 150 issues, most of which the court deemed frivolous.

The appellate court was so disgusted by the ridiculously excessive number of issues, it wrote in its decision upholding the convictions that the appellate defense attorney, Sara Webster, had egregiously violated her duty as an attorney. Justice Mitchell Goldberg was so infuriated that the court was forced to waste enormous public resources reviewing so many frivolous issues, he took the extraordinary step of recommending that the perpetrator *and his lawyer* be sanctioned. Judge Goldberg should get an award. Other judges should take a lesson.

Let's look at the even more shocking case of Debra Hagen, who may be the most violated and exploited victim in the history of our court system when it comes to delay tactics in criminal cases.

Debra was a young woman in her twenties in 1985 when she was brutally raped by a close family friend she called her "godfather," James Kelly. A jury found Kelly guilty of raping Debra in 1987 and Kelly was sentenced to serve ten years in state prison, but as of 2001, when Debra asked me to represent her, Kelly had yet to serve a single day behind bars.

Like many crime victims, Debra assumed the prosecutor was on her side. This was a big mistake, as Debra learned when the years went by and, despite many calls to the district attorney's office asking why her rapist had not yet started serving his sentence, Kelly remained a free man. Debra was initially told that Kelly couldn't go to prison because he was ill. Other times, it was because Kelly's appeal was still pending. Debra didn't know if any of this was true, but what could she do? The prosecutor just kept telling her not to worry; the legal process was simply running its dreadfully slow course.

Debra had faith in the system. She had done all the right things that were expected of her as a rape victim. She reported the crime to police right away. She went to the hospital where evidence was obtained and photographs were taken of the bruises on her neck where she had been strangled. She cooperated with law enforcement, waited patiently during the grueling pretrial period, and ultimately testified in front of a jury about all the horrible details.

When Kelly's trial wrapped up in 1987, the jury almost immediately found him guilty. The judge was prepared to pronounce sentence immediately, but Kelly appeared to become faint in the courtroom. Sentencing was put off and Kelly was admitted to a psychiatric ward at a local hospital.

Kelly finally showed up to receive his punishment months later, arriving by ambulance after conveniently scheduling his court appearance to coincide with another hospitalization for a minor medical procedure. The judge sentenced him to prison, but put a hold on Kelly's incarceration until he got out of the hospital. It was the government's job to have someone waiting to take Kelly to prison the minute he left the hospital. But that didn't happen, and a convicted rapist went home to freedom.

Debra called the prosecutor many times over the years to ask why Kelly was still free. In 1992, she even sent a letter to the judge seeking an explanation, but the judge passed it on to the prosecutor, and nothing happened.

The prosecution continued to do nothing for ten more years until police happened upon Kelly one day and realized he should have been behind bars. The local media caught on and started writing stories about the nearly fourteen-year delay. The elected prosecutor, District Attorney John Conte, knew his office was in trouble, and he was desperate to make the whole thing go away as quickly as possible.

When I came on board, Conte's office was already trying to get Debra to agree to a deal that would have allowed Kelly to remain a free man. If Debra complied with the deal, Conte could smooth everything over with the public by saying that he and the victim had reached an agreement.

To her eternal credit, Debra refused to be manipulated. She wanted Kelly to serve the sentence he had justly received - nothing more, nothing less. She also wanted some accountability for fourteen years of delay.

I agreed to represent Debra for free and filed a motion seeking enforcement of her right to a "prompt disposition." I asked the court to take custody of Kelly so he could start serving his sentence, and I insisted that the judge give Debra a full explanation for what took so long.

At the hearing on my motion, Kelly arrived in a wheelchair, slouched over and drooling. Though Kelly was by this time in his early 70s, and he looked feeble, I was suspicious because he'd made so many false claims about his poor health over the years.

The next day, a local newspaper that was in the tank for the district attorney published a front-page photo of Kelly in his wheelchair and wrote a sympathetic story claiming the guy had serious heart and lung problems, and implying that Debra was cruel for demanding that such a sick old man go to prison. That day, as I was preparing an appeal to the Massachusetts Supreme Judicial Court, I received a phone call from a State Trooper who told me that he'd seen Kelly's picture in the paper. He wanted me to know that he had run into Kelly days earlier at a courthouse, where the not so feeble rapist was seen walking around with his girlfriend, smoking and driving his car.

I was livid, but not shocked. And even if Kelly had been ill, so what? Criminals far sicker than Kelly pretended to be are sent to prison all the time. I once prosecuted an eighty-eight-year-old man for second-offense indecent assault on a child, a crime that carried a five-year mandatory minimum prison term. The disgusting geezer molested a child who was visiting her grandmother at the nursing home where he lived. He always came to court using a walker, and his lawyer complained to the judge that it was inhumane to put such an old man behind bars. Give me a break! If a child predator is healthy enough to coerce a little girl to fondle his genitals, he's more than healthy enough to have his whole evil body shipped off to prison - walker and all.

Growing doubts about Kelly's disabilities led a *Boston Herald* reporter, Jack Sullivan, to stake out Kelly's home. During the stakeout, Kelly was photographed smoking, weeding his garden, and taking out large bags of trash. No drooling, frail old man - just a fraud caught in the act.

Thanks to Jack Sullivan, the court and the public could finally see Kelly for the devious trickster he was, a master manipulator whose charade was being aided not only by his defense attorneys, but also by the prosecutor. I put the *Boston Herald's* story in my appellate brief and slammed the entire legal system for doing *nothing* to protect Debra's right to a "prompt disposition."

The Supreme Judicial Court scheduled a hearing on my appeal right around the time I was supposed to be giving birth to my fifth child. They offered two possible dates: August 8th and August 22nd. I requested August 8th and told the court I was due to give birth on August 13th. When the defense attorney and prosecutor learned that I'd asked for the 8th, they insisted on the 22nd. The case was getting much press attention, which was good for Debra. They knew that if I didn't show up, there would be less media coverage. The court assigned the case to be heard on August 22nd.

When August 13th rolled around and my baby hadn't yet arrived, I got nervous. Unlike the prosecutor and defense attorney who could send substitutes, I was working alone, for free, and there were fourteen years worth of case files. If I didn't make it to court, Debra would have no lawyer. By August 19th, I was desperate. If didn't give birth that day, and get out of the hospital two days later, I'd never get to court at 9 a.m. on August 22nd. I called my doctor and she agreed to induce me.

My perfectly cooked little darling arrived that night, and I got out of the hospital on the afternoon of August 21st. The next morning, I tugged on a maternity suit and brought my baby with me (along with two sitters) to court. Not only did the ploy to keep me out of the courtroom fail, we got double the press attention because I had a two and a-half day old baby in tow! I was exhausted and feeling pretty bad, but I rocked the case, and the other lawyers looked like idiots. The media tried to get me to pose for a photo-op with my baby, but I refused. I told them to focus on the grave injustice that Debra had endured.

Our strategy and dogged perseverance paid off! Debra won her case, and Kelly went to prison where he died, ironically enough, after developing a legitimate illness. Debra's case was a landmark ruling that changed the law to help all victims because the court held for the first time ever that victims must be afforded a right to *personally* address the court to demand speedy justice when their right to a "prompt disposition" is threatened or violated.

Debra's struggle is a tale of intimidation, lies, and blatant unfairness, facilitated by strategically engineered delays that almost succeeded in letting a convicted rapist avoid any punishment for the brutal rape of a young woman. What Debra did is what any one of us should do if faced with a similar situation: She spoke up, she stood firm, and she did not back down until justice was served. For fifteen years, Debra simply refused to believe that she had no choice but to accept Kelly's freedom. As you can probably tell, I have immense admiration for her strength and unwavering commitment to justice.

Yes, the Constitutional right to a speedy trial is important and must be defended vigorously. But until victims' speedy trial rights are respected, too, criminals and their lawyers will continue to make a mockery of the Constitution. Without blinking an eye, defense attorneys will drag out a victim's suffering for whatever strategic value they can get; and unless we do something about it, victims like Debra Hagen, and the integrity of law itself, will continue to suffer.

You can help ensure that prosecutors don't shirk their responsibilities the way John Conte did in Debra's case. One way is to form citizens' groups and organize protests to openly shame inept prosecutors. Bill O'Reilly did this to great effect when Atlanta District Attorney Paul Howard allowed a baby-murderer to choose a sentence of tubal ligation for the crime of murdering her own infant. No jail time. No punishment. No sanctions. She was sentenced to permanent birth control on the public's dime.

By shining a light on the case, O'Reilly helped the public learn a lot about the district attorney's low opinion of children's lives. This makes a big difference at reelection time when people who care about issues such as violence against women and children can join together and use their strength in numbers to force the election of a better prosecutor.

Despite the simplicity of this idea, it is a rarely used strategy. Why? In part, because most people have no idea who the elected prosecutor is in their jurisdiction. Law-abiding citizens don't think much about crime, so they don't focus on the race for district attorney, or understand why it matters to them in their everyday lives. As a result, prosecutors are usually elected based on meaningless things like name recognition and whether they won or lost any high profile cases.

Prosecutors also win or lose elections based on how much money they raise during the campaign, and guess who provides much of that financing? That's right, defense attorneys. There are exceptions, of course, and the defense bar doesn't have the same political cache in all fifty states, but victims have very little lobbying power in any jurisdiction. Maybe it's because few victims are comfortable joining groups whose common interest is that they suffered some horrible act of violence. People like to forget about pain.

Organizations like rape-crisis centers and battered-women's programs could help with political mobilization efforts, but they're usually afraid to criticize public officials for fear they might lose their government grant money, and they're often run by partisan ideologues who promote liberal, anti-prosecution ideas, so they're rarely helpful when it comes to holding prosecutors accountable for not doing right by victims.

We need more and better organized groups of people working together to make sure prosecutors are elected not because they show up on the nightly news, but because they exercise their discretion responsibly, and spend the public's money on the right priorities.

I know many of you care about these issues, even if crime has never directly affected your life. That's why I hope you'll get involved. Talk to your friends and neighbors about who's running for district attorney. Help people understand why it's important to vote for a particular candidate. At election time, ask the candidates tough questions about exactly how they plan to spend your tax dollars fighting the crimes that *you* care about, and how they will protect victims' rights. Then use your strength in numbers to spread the word about which prosecutor deserves to win, and why. Host community meetings, write letters to the editor for your local paper, buy billboards and newspapers ads if you can afford it, or put signs on your lawn. Think creatively. If you really, really wanted your best friend to win a political race in your town, what would you do to make sure they were elected?

If we don't get more involved, we'll get prosecutors like John Conte and Paul Howard every time. Our children won't be safe, injustice will prevail, and it will be our own fault.

SEVEN

Manipulating the Media

In chapter six, I introduced you to a particularly
objectionable character, the late James Kelly, a convicted
rapist who pretended to be an invalid to get his picture on
the front page of a local newspaper, so he could use the
media to help fend off his incarceration. Kelly isn't the only
bad guy who used the press to manipulate the court of
public opinion in an attempt to evade justice. The same
thing happened in the Scott Peterson, Kobe Bryant, and
Michael Jackson cases, circuses all, in which the media
trough was constantly filled with nonsense, much of which
was designed to distract the public by getting them focused
on less important, though more entertaining, sideshows.

In high-profile criminal cases, defense by dog-and-
pony-show tactics are commonplace because they're
effective, and because nothing meaningful can be done to
stop them. If a prosecutor lied to the public or tried to whip
people into a frenzy, sanctions would be flying, but defense
attorneys don't get in trouble. Here's why: Judges have
authority to punish prosecutors by excluding evidence or
even dismissing serious criminal charges when they say or
do something unfair to the accused. But a judge has no

authority to use the same sanctions against a defense attorney because sanctions might interfere with the accused's fair trial rights, and the court cannot punish a defendant for the bad behavior of his lawyer.

Even if a defense attorney makes false and derogatory public statements about a victim, judges can't really do anything about it, which is why so many defense lawyers blab on and on about whatever they please - truth and fairness to the victim be damned.

One more time: Prosecutors usually don't try to influence public opinion during the trial because they don't want the judge to toss out their evidence or dismiss the charges, but defense attorneys do all sorts of things to influence public opinion because there's virtually nothing the judge can do to stop them.

This is why during the Michael Jackson trial, for example, the prosecutor said very little to the media while Jackson had no qualms about dancing on top of cars outside the courthouse and showing up in pajamas. Who can forget that scene? Jackson in flannel PJs, hair all crooked, doing something that resembled the "Thorazine shuffle." He looked like a pathetic underfed psycho. Most thought the scene was a staged attempt to persuade the jury that Jackson was too frail to go to prison.

It's strange to think a guy like Jackson would want that kind of sympathy, and maybe he really was sick. But come on, people about to drop dead from cancer at least put their pants on before they go to court. Most normal defendants wouldn't want to look like a crazy person because it doesn't usually win you many friends on the jury. But when you're Michael Jackson, and there's much evidence against you (a credible victim, your own confession that you slept with children, police finding porn and booze in your bedroom, and testimony that you've molested several other boys in the past), the jury might just give you a break if they think you're not so much dangerous as a hopelessly strange dude.

Whatever one thinks of Jackson's behavior with kids, he didn't deserve to die, and the monster doctor who anesthetized him to death was rightly convicted of manslaughter. But Jackson's death changes nothing about the fact that he should never have escaped responsibility for the things he did to children. And who knows, maybe a stint behind bars would have saved his life. Maybe, he would have gotten the treatment he needed to address the suffering he endured as a child, and figure out how to stop himself from hurting others.

It's an interesting question for Jackson's defense team because while they may well feel good that they won Jackson's freedom in the sex abuse trial, they may also be responsible for setting Jackson on a course of self-destruction that ultimately had the guy demanding dangerous doses of anesthesia to go to sleep. Maybe being held accountable in a court of law would have helped the guy find a less lethal pathway to peace of mind.

While Michael Jackson will never again be accused of harming a child, his successful efforts to manipulate the legal system into producing an unjust acquittal will not soon be forgotten. All prosecutors should take a lesson because another superstar will one day be accused of similar crimes, and the public has a right to expect a better result.

Between now and then, we can all be a little more suspicious when we see Jackson-like games being played on the courthouse steps by remembering that the defense can do whatever it wants to spin the evidence and lie to the public, while the prosecution is forced to fight with both hands tied behind their backs.

Let's examine how another defendant used the media to manipulate public opinion with lies. In 2004, Scott Peterson was charged with murdering his wife, Laci, and their unborn son. Peterson's lawyer, Mark Geragos, knew the public was riveted by the story, and he used the press to distort the truth. During the trial, he repeatedly made crazy claims that had little or no basis in reality, but he knew they would make big headlines. One week, it was a claim about a new DNA test that would identify the real killer. Another time, it was a new mystery witness who could prove Scott's innocence. Of course, none of this ever developed into anything, but Geragos knew exactly how to infect the news cycle by focusing people on the fake "bombshells," to distract them from the prosecution's real and mounting evidence. Not surprisingly, the fake "bombshells" were often released to the media toward the end of the week to ensure that the entire weekend of cable news reporting and punditry would be devoted to analysis of the lies rather than the unpleasant *real* evidence of Peterson's guilt.

Peterson's lawyers had an advantage that doesn't exist in low profile trials because we were all so riveted by the seeming mystery of it all, and this effect was only magnified by the guy's icy-cold demeanor. How could a man who killed his pregnant wife and nearly born son at Christmastime be so cool? Wouldn't a guilty person be a withering mess? Being riveted by a mystery is fine, being riveted by lies is not. Our reluctance to believe that Peterson was capable of such hideous violence helped some people latch on to ridiculous theories about what happened. (Remember the tale about the devil worshippers in the van?) And even as we came to see with clarity how vicious Scott Peterson really was, we still couldn't look away because then we wanted to know *how* and *why* he did it.

The why became clear when we learned about Amber Frey, but the how remains a big unknown even today, though I have my theory:

Laci's body was discovered dressed in the pants she'd been wearing the night of the murder, and a maternity bra, but the shirt she'd had on was found in her laundry basket. In other words, she was apparently half undressed, getting ready for bed, when she was killed. When Scott was taken in for questioning, he had cuts on the knuckles of three fingers on his left hand. This suggests that Laci was strangled to death from behind, perhaps right after she took off her shirt. My theory is that Scott sneaked up behind his very pregnant wife and grabbed her by the throat with both hands. As she struggled to breathe, Laci did what any of us would have done if we were being strangled from behind: She reached up with her right hand (she was right-handed) in an attempt to rip Scott's fingers off her neck. As Laci fought to breathe, she pulled hard, scraping her fingernails (pregnant women have *very* strong fingernails) down the knuckles of Scott's left hand in a failed effort to release his grip. Scott told cops he cut his knuckles on a toolbox in his truck, but tests on the toolbox showed there was no DNA or blood anywhere.

You might not buy this theory, but it makes a hell of a lot more sense than some of the crazy things the defense was saying about Laci being kidnapped by a satanic cult. Yet we heard about the cult theory almost every day during the Peterson trial, and we heard almost nothing about Scott's scraped knuckles or the significance of Laci's half-dressed body.

Red-herring defense strategies are among the most serious problems in our legal system today. Why? Because the public thinks criminal trials are a search for the truth, and the unending stream of false revelations feeds right into this myth. Good, we think to ourselves, they're really digging deep into the facts and the evidence. In reality, the defense isn't searching for the truth so much as a way to bury it. When truth is irrelevant, and winning is the only goal, lawyers are free to use all kinds of distortion strategies, including the dissemination of outright lies, no matter who the lies hurt and no matter how much harm is done to the integrity of law itself.

One of the most vicious distortion tactics I've ever seen reared its ugly head in the Kobe Bryant case. Like hearing the sound of fingernails on a chalkboard, I was nearly debilitated when defense attorney Pamela Mackey asked in open court on October 9, 2003, whether the victim's vaginal injuries were consistent with her having "sex with three men in three days." It was obviously intended as a distraction tactic, but would the general public figure that out? Would anyone even ask how the defense arrived at the number three? I did. And you won't believe the outrageous answer.

First, they counted Bryant's sexual assault (hardly counts as sex). Then they counted a consensual interlude between the victim and her boyfriend two days before the assault (fair enough, though irrelevant). Then they counted an incident that simply never occurred at all. What, you ask? They counted an imaginary incident? Yes, this alleged third incident grew out of the discovery of unidentified microscopic sperm cells that did not match Bryant's DNA. The defense theory was that the sperm were deposited when the victim had sex with someone after the rape on her way home from the hotel.

The absurdity of this claim should have prevented anyone with a brain from repeating it as if true. I'm not saying it's impossible for anyone ever to have consensual sex during the drive home after being raped. But there was no evidence that such an event happened, and unidentified DNA proved nothing. Let me tell you why.

The mystery DNA consisted of dead sperm cells with no tails. A whopping total of four dead sperm from the mystery man were found inside the victim's body. Better yet, there was no semen! Given that one ejaculation produces million and millions of sperm, *and* that they need a ride to get out of the body (that's what semen is for), *and* that they live for up to five days (tails fall off when they die), the old and dead nature of the sperm, plus the fact that only four were found in the victim's body, is indisputable evidence that there was no post-rape sex. District Attorney Mark Hurlbert told me the "mystery" DNA found on the victim was all old and dead, from the same person - most likely the victim's boyfriend - and most certainly from an encounter weeks earlier. But this didn't inhibit a defense expert named Dr. Elizabeth Johnson from stating under oath "to a reasonable degree of scientific certainty," that the dead sperm evidence was "consistent with" the victim having sex after Bryant's attack and before she went to the hospital early the next day.

The lie about sex-with-three-men-in-three-days worked wonders to distract the public from paying any attention to all the damning evidence that had come out in court earlier that day. The allegations were gruesome, that Bryant grabbed the victim by the neck, bent her over a chair, raped her from behind with such force and friction her genital area tore and started bleeding. (The injury had nothing to do with Bryant's size, a racist myth bandied about during the case.) The victim's blood was found on the underside of Bryant's T-shirt, and he reportedly admonished her not to tell anyone what happened before sending her away like a piece of trash.

With facts like those, the defense needed more than a red herring to distract the public, and they didn't have it, so they created it out of whole cloth. The sex-with-three-men-in-three-days announcement was so shocking to most people, it was far more than a red herring, it was a neon scarlet killer whale because it had all the salacious qualities that would make a sex-crazed public sit up and take notice. And it was exactly the type of evidence the hungry Bryant fan club was aching for, the kind of information they could latch on to that would help them feel better about rooting for a superstar athlete instead of a traumatized rape victim.

For months thereafter, the mainstream news media and almost every pundit on the planet, myself and a couple of others excluded, repeated the lie. Whenever I was asked on a news show about the victim having sex with three men in three days, I would take a deep breath and respond: "Bryant bent her over a chair, raped her from behind, and tore her genital area, leaving her blood on his T-shirt, etc." The host would brush off my answer and say something like, "Well, okay, Wendy, that's all well and good, but let's talk about the sex-with-three-men-in-three-days issue."

Again, I'd take a deep breath, roll my eyes, and say, "He bent her over a chair . . ." And so on, and so on. I knew the game, and I wasn't playing.

Even more shocking than the lie about the victim having sex with three men in three days was what happened when the victim's lawyer tried to correct the lie by issuing a statement to the media dismissing the claim as false. The judge, Terry Ruckriegle, hauled him into court and threatened him with contempt for violating the gag order. Mind you, Ruckriegle didn't even have authority to punish a lawyer who wasn't directly involved in the criminal trial, but that didn't stop him. And he never so much as admonished Pamela Mackey for lying about the victim's sexual conduct, or for any of the other outrageous things Mackey did, like "accidentally" identifying the victim by name repeatedly in open court. Calling the victim by her real name wouldn't be such a big deal if she hadn't repeatedly been threatened with death by Bryant sycophants, but Judge Ruckriegle didn't seem to care. A better judge would have held Mackey in contempt, or at least filed ethical charges against her. He did neither.

Let's be clear about this: When the victim's lawyer told the truth, he was threatened with contempt, but when Bryant's lawyer lied, nothing happened. Judge Ruckriegle should apologize to the victim and to the public, but don't hold your breath.

Kobe Bryant was a popular guy and an excellent athlete at the time he was charged with rape. He was worth a fortune to the Lakers. He was also a very wealthy man which enabled him to hire a team of expensive lawyers. But Bryant's case wasn't dismissed because of great lawyering. Any idiot can make up lies. It was dismissed because Mackey stooped very, very low to make sure the truth was not told and that the Lakers could hold on to their star shooting guard.

At least it's over now and all is well with the world, right? Not exactly. Criminals everywhere (along with their lawyers) learned a few lessons from Bryant's high-priced tricksters. Thanks to the defense-at-any-cost nonsense in Bryant's case, it seems a safe bet that this sort of vile lawyering will be coming soon to a courthouse near you soon. Nice.

For my part, I'm not waiting for the next circus. I'm fighting right now for new laws that will explicitly authorize victims and their lawyers to speak publicly, without threat of contempt, whenever a false statement is made about a victim. We also need rules that will immediately strip lawyers of their licenses to practice law, forever, if they make false public statements that expose victims to an increased risk of serious violence during a criminal case.

And we need more education about the deceptive things defense attorneys get away with in the name of justice. Jurors in the courtroom, and those in the court of public opinion, have to start assessing information they receive from defense lawyers with an appropriate level of skepticism. Think about all the things we've learned to be skeptical about - like whether the jelly people paid for a study that "proves" marshmallow fluff is bad for kids because they want to be peanut butter's exclusive sandwich partner. We should be skeptical of well-timed media bombshells in criminal cases, too.

And the media has to start doing a better job writing about criminal cases. Journalism is supposed to be about truth. But in court, winning is the only goal, especially for the defense. Given this reality, the media should take extra care not to simply report what the defense says, and then let the other side be quoted as saying it's not true. This isn't good enough because the defense has far more freedom than the prosecution does to misstate the truth, which makes it journalistically irresponsible to publish a lie so long as someone denies it because the very act of publication creates the false sense that there's at least a fifty-fifty chance the lie is true, and some consumers of news will choose to believe it.

Defense attorneys are right to complain that prosecutors use the media, too, especially when they leak grand jury evidence before charges are filed. But let's be honest. While prosecutors leak, defense attorneys gush. And though leaks are bad, lies are worse. Journalists know that unlike grand jury testimony, statements made by defense counsel in court are not reliable because they aren't under oath and aren't subject to any preliminary scrutiny for truthfulness. That Mackey's comment was supported by the claims set forth in an "expert" affidavit makes no difference because the law does not prohibit hired guns from filing false affidavits in court.

The misuse of media as a tool by which criminal lawyers dump false information into the court of public opinion is way out of control. But we can all do something about it by checking facts ourselves, using the Internet and blog sites to share information and by talking with others about the truth. We can write letters to the editor when the media gets it wrong and simply be more skeptical consumers of news. The longer we wait to start holding the media accountable, the greater the chance that public cynicism about the criminal justice system will start to infect print journalism, known as the "fourth estate." Call me a doomsayer, but considering the financial struggles of most newspapers these days, the press doesn't need more reasons for people to be suspicious about how they do their job.

EIGHT

Picking Dumb Jurors

There's no polite way to say what's coming next, so I'll just plunge ahead: Distortion tactics work particularly well when the jury's collective IQ hovers somewhere around dumb as a rock.

Only the dimmest of jurors buy into the kinds of crazy antics that are designed to divert their attention away from the real evidence. So it should come as no surprise that defense attorneys generally try to pick dopes during jury selection. Yes, there are exceptions to this rule but on the whole, dummies are good for an unscrupulous defense attorney who hopes to persuade a jury to ignore the obvious, abandon common sense, and vote not guilty. Sure, sometimes even smart jurors act like idiots, but few people with true intelligence can be tricked into acquitting a clearly guilty criminal. Defense attorneys know that one nitwit is all it takes, so the hunt for nitwits is a big part of the game.

It's embarrassing, I know. And nobody is doing anything about it.

Ever since the O. J. verdict in 1995, dumb-juror syndrome has been on the rise. Lawyers everywhere learned about the power of stupid, and jury consultants developed psychological sonar to identify idiots in the sea of citizens who show up for jury duty. Is it any wonder that today we see so many acquittals in the face of overwhelming evidence?

We've all heard the stories about how people get out of jury duty, but did you know that some jurors go out of their way to get chosen for certain types of cases, especially high-profile trials. Even a dummy can be smart enough to know that there might be fame and fortune ahead if they get picked for a big case. Whether the motivation is to sell a book or just enjoy fifteen minutes of fame, the jury system is awash in a flood of brainless morons. Sorry if this sounds harsh, but it has to be said because it's a real problem.

And if having a lot of numbskulls on juries isn't bad enough, there's mounting evidence of a problem that I call lying-juror syndrome.

During a murder trial in Boston in 2004, it was uncovered during deliberations that five out of twelve jurors lied under oath during the screening process about whether they had ever been convicted of a crime. Not one, or two, but almost *half* of the jurors in a single case *lied* about their criminal records, even though they'd been warned that they could get in serious trouble if they didn't tell the truth.

Despite significant public outrage about the case, none of the jurors was punished, which sends a terrible message about whether we have a right to expect jurors to act with integrity. It's not that people with rap sheets should never sit on juries. Some of the best jurors are people with street smarts who understand the way bad guys do business. But can't we at least agree that people who commit perjury during jury selection might not be the pick of the litter when it comes to building public confidence in the system.

And get this: The lawyer for the guy who was on trial for murder when the lying jurors got caught had the audacity to complain to the judge that the prosecutor who found out the truth should be sanctioned for violating the jurors' privacy rights. Think about that: The defense attorney argued that the prosecutor had no business looking at the jurors' criminal records to determine whether they lied because the records were confidential.

This is what we've come to. Defense lawyers arguing with a straight face that convicted felons have a right to lie with impunity when they show up for jury duty. Criminals lie, jurors lie, defense attorneys lie, and that's O.K., but we're supposed to accept that when a prosecutor finds out the *truth* about a juror's rap sheet, he should be punished for violating the juror's privacy. What's that saying about the nuts running the asylum?

Speaking of nuts, some jurors aren't stupid so much as smitten, because they get goo-goo eyes for the lawyers. This was the syndrome du jour during the William Kennedy Smith rape trial, when one idiot fell for Smith's lawyer, Roy Black. She voted not guilty and then married the guy after the case was over. All I can say is, too bad the assistant district attorney didn't look like Pamela Anderson. If these are the things that drive jurors' decisions, maybe a sex-crazed male juror would have voted guilty in the hope of getting a date with the prosecutor. At least there would have been balance to the craziness.

Then there's the celebrity factor. Whatever else jurors suffer from generally, there is no rational explanation for the not-guilty verdict in the Michael Jackson case except that besides being dumb, the jurors couldn't think straight because they were starry-eyed about Jackson's fame. This might be called the stupid-and-celebrity-crazed-juror syndrome. If the perpetrator is a beloved, famous somebody in this country, and he commits a crime, he'll never see a day behind bars - assuming, of course, that his defense team picks enough jurors who are so hopelessly smitten they're literally unable look at and listen to the evidence because they're only thinking about getting an autograph.

This is apparently what happened with the prosecution of Michael Jackson. Jackson simply was too popular, and some might say too pathetic, to convict. We probably shouldn't overlook the fact that he put the struggling town of Santa Maria, California, on the map, too. Perhaps it was wishful thinking to expect that they would ever send their only claim to fame to prison.

The fact that the jurors in the Jackson case got it so badly wrong on the world stage and so soon after the O. J. Simpson debacle makes the loss a colossal embarrassment for all Americans. As I said in the introduction, we like to brag to other countries that we have the best system on the planet. But then, in a couple of high-profile cases where the evidence of guilt is overwhelming and the perps walk free, we show our true colors, and they are not pretty.

The Simpson verdict was painful enough, but the Jackson verdict - yeesh! What did the jurors *think* Jackson was doing with the jar of Vaseline next to the porn on the night table next to the bed where, according to one of Jackson's own witnesses, the pop singer boasted about sleeping with one little boy *365 times*? This is not rocket science.

Maybe we can take a little comfort from the fact that a few jurors in the Jackson case had an after-the-fact epiphany about how wrong they had been. They described not just pressure but outright bullying by other jurors to render a not-guilty verdict. One said jurors were told they would be removed from the case if they did not vote to acquit. Another said he was lied to by other jurors who told him the law *required* them to vote not guilty if they had even a tiny bit of doubt. The truth is, jurors can and should find a defendant guilty even if they have doubt - as long as the doubt is not "unreasonable." The bully jurors and the ones who lied about the definition of reasonable doubt should have been punished, or at least removed from the jury before the verdict was decided.

When jurors are idiots, they can't rise above their own cloudy vision of the world, so they make unfair judgments based on social stereotypes. And while judges in most states are required to instruct jurors not to be biased toward "either party," this doesn't help victims and witnesses because they're not "parties" to the criminal case. In other words, jurors are told to be fair to the accused, but not the victim or anyone else.

Great. No wonder the jurors were so quick to blame the mother of Michael Jackson's victim for their not guilty verdict. She may well have been a troubled soul, but almost every scandalous thing we heard about her was completely irrelevant. The jurors clearly did not understand this given that one said she voted not guilty, in part, because she didn't like the victim's mother. This juror literally said, "What kind of mother would let her son sleep at Michael Jackson's house?"

I let this woman have it when I was doing commentary on TV after the verdict. What kind of juror votes not guilty because of how they feel about a victim's mother?! Why didn't the idiot have the common sense to know that even if the victim's mother laid her son out naked on Jackson's bed, the twisted pop star had absolutely no right to touch that poor child. And, furthermore, if she thought the victim's mother was a bad parent for letting her son sleep at Jackson's house, doesn't that mean she believed Jackson was dangerous to young boys?

The sad fact is that because common sense and integrity are not required for jury duty, the system is in deep trouble. I recall a child rape case I prosecuted where a teacher was selected to serve on the jury. I thought he would be fair because teachers understand kids, but the teacher voted not guilty on one of the charges (guilty on the other) and explained after the verdict that he believed the child about the first assault, but not the second, because the child may have learned how to lie about rape when she was being abused the first time. An educated juror, yes, but clearly an idiot.

There are glimmers of hope. A jury from the area around Cambridge, Massachusetts had tons of common sense when they voted to convict Louise Woodward of murder in 1997 for the brutal shaking and beating death of baby Matthew Eappen. That high-profile case, known as the "Nanny Trial," was dominated by multi-syllabic blather from one defense expert after the next who went on for days about how the baby suffered a minor bump on the head long before he died, and that a small injury had grown over time and exploded when Woodward just happened to be alone with the child. It felt like a dense scientific fog was settling in to suffocate the truth in the courtroom.

But the stark backdrop against which this fog rolled in was that no child in the history of humanity had ever died in the way the defense experts said Matty Eappen had died. The jury smartly ignored the defense experts and believed the medical professionals who tried to save Matty Eappen's life - experts who were not paid a fortune for their testimony and who said the baby had all the earmarks of having been shaken violently and slammed against a hard surface. The injuries included subdural bleeding between the brain and the skull, perimacular (accordion-like) folds in the retinas, and a two and a-half inch-long skull fracture.

The jury kept hold of common sense despite the defense lawyers' dog-and-pony show (paid for by EF Au Pair, the agency that selected Woodward to care for Matty Eappen and that would have benefited greatly in a civil suit had there been a not guilty verdict) and found Woodward guilty of murder.

Woodward's lawyer, Barry Sheck, whined after the guilty verdict that the jury wasn't smart enough to understand the complicated scientific evidence. I laughed when I heard this. "Barry's just a sore loser," I said on one television program. "The truth is, he tried but couldn't find enough dopes to stuff on a jury in Cambridge, Massachusetts."

In fact, dumb jurors are everywhere. Stated differently, you can wind up with dumb or deranged jurors no matter where the case is tried because in most states, lawyers aren't allowed to ask jurors the kinds of questions that might reveal whether they are competent to serve.

A couple of years ago, one of my students told me about her experience as a juror. During deliberations in the case, she noticed one very quiet juror who seemed pensive and thoughtful, while others droned on annoyingly about the evidence. Eventually, she sought out the quiet guy's opinion, but he didn't reply - not because he was thoughtful, but because he didn't speak English. The guy not only couldn't answer her question, he hadn't understood what the witnesses were saying when they took the stand.

We clearly need new laws that mandate better juror screening to eliminate people who are unwilling to listen or incapable of understanding the evidence. For the results of jury trials to be worthy of the public's respect, we need jurors to bring at least a baseline of intelligence and common sense to the process. And we must ensure that jurors are instructed to be fair not only to the accused, but also to victims and witnesses.

We also need swift and strong punishments for jurors who lie about their criminal records. When the public hears that a juror went to jail for lying, the news will spread like wildfire, and everyone will get the message loud and clear: Jury duty is serious business.

This country has a very generous Bill of Rights, but there's no such thing as a Constitutional right to select dumb jurors. New laws will take much work and defense attorneys will fiercely resist any attempt to improve the quality of jury selection policies, but it's a worthy battle.

Remember (Wendy) Murphy's Law. The craziness will only continue if we let it. We can't develop a pill to make every juror competent, but we have to pay more attention to the ones who are not qualified, and do something to keep them away from our courthouses.

NINE

Exploiting Victims' Fears

The meanest trick of all is when defense lawyers negotiate bargain-basement plea deals or otherwise gain strategic advantages by exploiting a victim's fears. The most despicable example is when defense attorneys in child-abuse cases invoke the argument that a plea bargain will protect the child from the trauma of testifying.

It's a very appealing argument. Who wouldn't want to protect a child victim from pain? The problem is, kids don't necessarily suffer when they testify, but parents of victims don't know any better, so when someone tells them that testifying will be bad for the child, they'll take any plea deal to make the whole horrible thing go away.

The harsh realities of the justice system, made harsh in part by unrestrained defense tactics, have become a powerful weapon in the game of plea-bargaining. More than just making kids afraid of testifying, the defense gets to negotiate discounts by doing things like refusing to reveal their HIV status unless the victim agrees to a sentence of probation.

And who can forget the disgusting, bottom-feeding lawyers for David Westerfield, the man convicted in 2002 of murdering little seven-year old Danielle Van Dam, who tried to negotiate the most vile deal ever conceived. Get this: Attorneys Steven Feldman and Robert Boyce offered to reveal the location of Danielle's dead body in exchange for the prosecution agreeing to drop its plan to seek the death penalty.

Thankfully, the child's body was uncovered before the deal was made. But think about that: Should a child murderer *ever* get a discount because the victim's parents are desperate to find the remains of their little girl? Is there a more inhumane way to run a justice system?

Westerfield's lawyers will never rid themselves of the shame they deserve for even trying to broker such a deal. Both men will hopefully fail the pillows-and-mirror test for the rest of their lives - meaning that if they each have a conscience, they won't sleep well and won't be able to look at themselves in the mirror without feeling sick.

Scaring kids and parents away from justice is just as wrong, but this is exactly what happened in the case of Rhode Island elementary-school principal, church volunteer, and Little League coach John W. Card. Card admitted in court to sexually abusing a child repeatedly over a period of several years. He was charged with forty-eight offenses against a male student, including rape. Under a plea bargain with the attorney general's office, Card pleaded guilty to only one count of second-degree child molestation and was set free on a suspended sentence. The rationale for this ridiculously lenient sentence was that the victim did not want to testify at trial. Not surprisingly, Card waited until the eve of trial to plead guilty - when his victim's fears and anxieties were at their peak - before using the intimidating nature of the system to demand a deep discount.

A similar save-the-child theme was in the air when John Andrews, the attorney for child rapist and rampant Massachusetts pedophile Christopher Reardon, claimed in 2002 that his client was pleading guilty on the eve of trial to "spare the children" the pain of testifying. Reardon, a church and community volunteer, had been indicted on 150 counts of sexual abuse and related crimes against nearly twenty children. A few weeks before trial, the victims' parents submitted affidavits explaining that their children were ready to testify but would be severely traumatized if their testimony were subjected to televised coverage. The defense objected. When the parents' efforts to keep the TV cameras out failed, Reardon agreed to plead guilty on the eve of trial, but only after the prosecution offered to reduce the number of charges by half to approximately seventy-five.

If Attorney Andrews really wanted to spare the children, he wouldn't have objected to the parents' request to keep cameras out. And if the perpetrator really gave a damn about his victims, he could have pled guilty long before the eve of trial. Keep in mind that these kids were teenagers at the time of trial, a difficult, busy, and turbulent phase of life. Reardon and his lawyer made these kids suffer needlessly, every day, thinking about how the grotesque things Reardon did to them would soon be on televised display for all their friends to see, in lurid detail.

Nobody did anything to stop Reardon's attorney from exploiting the victims' fears for whatever value he could extract during plea-bargain negotiations. Shameful, all around.

Even those who sincerely have victims' best interest at heart sometimes give away the store on tough punishments because they think it's important to protect children from testifying. Texas Judge G. Timothy Boswell sentenced forty-six-year-old police officer Richard Wilson to probation as part of a plea bargain after Wilson was charged with raping and abusing three girls and one boy. The prosecutor, Marcus Taylor, went along with the plea bargain because a therapist believed it was not in the best interest of one of the victims to testify. This was a curious excuse given that all the victims had testified at the first trial, which ended in a mistrial after one of the victims recanted her testimony.

(Note: recantations are usually false.) If it was in the kids' best interest to testify at the first trial when they were even younger, how did it suddenly become *not* in their best interest at the second trial when they were older?

If a child is legitimately too traumatized to testify but has given statements in an earlier trial or other legal proceeding, the judge should *never* allow a plea bargain, but instead should permit the prosecutor to substitute for the child's live testimony a transcript of what the child said at that earlier proceeding. This is permissible under the Constitution if the child is psychologically unable to testify so long as the defense had had a prior opportunity to conduct cross-examination.

The transcript of the child's prior testimony can also be admitted as evidence even if there was no opportunity for cross-examination if the perpetrator *caused the child to become unavailable* to testify. This so-called forfeiture-by-wrongdoing rule is an excellent though underutilized idea that allows all kinds of hearsay evidence to be used against the accused, even if it would otherwise violate his Constitutional rights, because a perpetrator forfeits his rights when he causes a victim to become too afraid to take the stand.

In many cases, a prosecutor can also win without putting the child on the stand by using things like medical records and statements the child made to a doctor or a parent. It's also very easy to prove a case without the victim if a 911 call was made at a time when the person making the call was upset about the crime. The "excited utterance" rule allows the tape to be admitted, and many cases are successfully prosecuted using only 911 tapes as evidence, even if the victim never shows up in court.

And let's not forget that perpetrators often confess, or at least admit to some aspects of the crime. Statements from the accused are usually admissible and are especially powerful evidence that can help prove the charges whether the victim takes the stand or not.

The best prosecutors know how to piece together a case with or without a victim. The crummy ones make deals, then blame victims for why they couldn't get the job done. Massachusetts District Attorneys Martha Coakley and Gerry Leone refused to prosecute a man accused of child sex abuse in 2005 and 2009 respectively. Child protective services investigated, credited the kids, and sent the cases to the prosecutor's office, but both times the guy was set free. That man, John Burbine, then went on to rape and abuse more than a dozen children, to whom he gained access through his wife's babysitting business. One of Burbine's victims was only *eight days-old*.

When Burbine was finally caught again, in 2012, and ultimately charged with dozens of sexual abuse and child pornography crimes, Leone explained that the 2005 and 2009 cases were not prosecuted, primarily to spare the victims the trauma of testifying. He never mentioned that *filing* charges in those cases would probably have spared Burbine's next twelve victims the trauma of being raped.

We need to start presuming that children, like adults, will be expected to testify in child abuse cases, not because we want them to be harmed, but out of respect for their rights as citizens. Kids are very good witnesses, primarily because they're not good liars. It's time we respected children enough to let their strong voices be heard.

If a psychologist determines that a child would be harmed by taking the stand, it might be appropriate not to force the issue. But while it is undoubtedly true that the well-being of a child is more important than prosecution, it is also true that the well-being of a child is not usually at risk when save-the-child plea bargains are struck.

Noted researcher Gail Goodman, a professor of psychology at the University of California at Davis, studied the well-being of twenty-seven child victims who testified in sexual-abuse cases. She found that many showed emotional improvement after testifying. In a similar group of children who were not required to testify, Goodman interviewed the victims as adults and found that many were expressing regret, saying things like, "I wish I could have testified." These data suggest that while the value of confronting an abuser in court may not appear clear to a child at the time of their testimony, there is obviously a psychological benefit and a feeling of empowerment for most children who participate in criminal trials.

Consider, for example, an eight-year-old client of mine who was repeatedly sexually assaulted by a babysitter. At first, his parents didn't want him to testify. They'd been told it would be a terrible experience, and they didn't want to put their son through it. But by the time of trial, they felt differently. The boy took the stand and did a great job testifying about all the horrible details. The jury found the perpetrator not guilty, in part because the child couldn't remember all the details of the crimes perfectly. No child ever does, nor do most adults.

Years later, his mother asked him how he felt about the experience. He responded, "I remember sitting in the big chair next to the judge. I was scared and I could see the bad guy staring at me, so I looked at the American Flag. There was a gold eagle on the top, so I just stared at the eagle. I felt strong and proud of myself, just like an eagle, because I told the truth."

Not all kids feel the same way, and most won't understand that it's an empowering experience until they're old enough to appreciate complex ideas, like justice. But the adults in charge of our legal system should consider Gail Goodman's research before letting another dangerous predator walk free on the theory that kids need to be "protected" from justice.

All children are at greater risk of harm when a dangerous predator is inadequately punished. The strong arm of the government is supposed to force reluctant witnesses to testify in serious criminal proceedings, simply because the system cannot work otherwise, and crime will flourish if we let victims choose not to participate.

If you're wondering how bad a trial might be for a child, you should know that defense attorneys can't get away with harshly questioning a young victim who takes the stand. There's too great a risk the jury won't like it and will hold it against the accused. I've never seen a defense attorney go after a child, and make no mistake about it, perpetrators are far more afraid of kids taking the stand than the children are afraid to testify because when a child does testify, the verdict is usually a fast vote of "guilty!"

It's time to hold prosecutors accountable for making deals on the backs of kids. We need to start electing district attorneys who are willing to open the doors to justice a little wider for children. No more automatic plea bargains to "spare" the victim the trauma of testifying. And if a perpetrator engages in scare tactics with the child or his family, prosecutors should file witness intimidation and obstruction-of-justice charges. If a defense attorney does something to intimidate a child, the prosecutor (or the child's parents) should file an ethics complaint with the bar.

Finally, all prosecutors should immediately announce to the public the adoption of a "no drop/no deal" policy in child-abuse cases. Perpetrators will be less inclined to engage in intimidation tactics if they know it won't win them any discounts.

Yes, the cost of a "no drop/no deal" policy includes the possibility that a few children will be upset when they're forced to testify, but remember; testifying doesn't necessarily traumatize children, and is often psychologically beneficial. And because 95 percent of all criminal cases end with guilty pleas anyway, few kids will ever be called to take the stand.

The key is to make sure children feel strong, willing and ready to testify, especially on the morning of trial. Most perpetrators will cave and plead guilty the minute they see their little victim walk through the courtroom door.

We owe kids this aggressive approach because we've never really done right by children in this country. We had laws on the books to protect animals from abuse long before we had laws to protect children. How can this be true, you wonder? I'm sure it's because a couple of hundred years ago, we thought animals were more valuable than kids. Shocking, I know. And we've certainly improved since then, but we bear the legacy of that ugliness in our legal system, and it shows every time we give out discounts to child predators. One researcher found that, on average, a homicide of a child receives one-fourth the punishment the same offense would carry if committed against an adult. This is unacceptable because it devalues children's lives and creates an incentive for criminals to target defenseless kids as their victims.

How about we get tough on child abuse for a change? It will never happen if we continue to tolerate a legal system rife with toothless laws and minimal enforcement efforts. Remember (Wendy) Murphy's Law? They can't get away with disrespecting kids if we don't let them.

TEN

Using the Cross-Fingerpointing Maneuver

One of the most frustrating situations for cops is when they know for certain that two people were present at the scene of a crime but only one of them is guilty, and neither of them is talking. Usually, this happens when the guilty person persuades the innocent one that if they stick together, neither one can successfully be prosecuted because they can each claim that the other one committed the crime.

I call this the cross-finger pointing trick because the case is virtually unprovable so long as the innocent buddy agrees to serve as the guilty person's built-in reasonable doubt.

Defense attorneys love this trick. And they have a sarcastic saying that sums up the tactic nicely: "Nobody talks, everybody walks." Many times it's public defenders pulling the stunt - which means *your* tax dollars at work.

In gang-violence cases when suspects try to get everyone to clam up, cops can sometimes pressure at least one suspect to roll on the others. But when there are only two suspects, and they're family members, police have a tougher time getting access to either one alone to solicit the truth.

In Florida, law enforcement officials have long been frustrated in their efforts to solve the 1997 disappearance and possible murder of "baby Sabrina." Sabrina's parents, Steve and Marlene Eisenberg, have denied any involvement in the crime, but have not been cleared. One explanation for why no charges have been filed is that police believe one of them is responsible, but if they pursue charges against the mother, for example, she can point the finger at the father, and vice versa.

Similarly, the murder of Martha Moxley in Greenwich, Connecticut in 1975 went unsolved for two decades. Police knew that one of two brothers from the Skakel family (celebrated Kennedy-related neighbors of the victim) was likely responsible for Moxley's death, but they could not be certain that a trial against either one would be successful because each brother could demonstrate reasonable doubt by pointing a finger at the other. Tommy Skakel was the last person seen with Moxley, but there was evidence implicating Michael Skakel, too.

Michael was eventually tried and convicted in 2002, after making enough damning statements about his involvement to tip the scales firmly in favor of prosecution. Unexpectedly, and to the credit of either the Skakel family or Michael's attorney, Mickey Sherman, Michael did not falsely point the finger at Tommy during trial.

In a more recent example of a possible cross-finger pointing problem, the Colorado parents of Jason Midyette were under the umbrella of suspicion for more than a year after their baby became seriously injured and died in March 2006. When medical professionals asked what happened, the parents hired criminal defense lawyers and clammed up. Obviously, law enforcement was suspicious, but when parents are the only ones who had ongoing access to the baby, and they stick together like glue, how can police ever prove which one did what?

The most famous cross-finger pointing case, interestingly enough coming out of the same jurisdiction as the Midyette case (Boulder, Colorado), is surely that of JonBenet Ramsey, the six-year-old little girl who was murdered and sexually assaulted in her own home on Christmas night in 1996. Most people believe that one of the parents, John or Patsy, killed JonBenet; and if this is true, the cross-finger pointing trick could explain why neither parent was ever charged with a crime.

While John and Patsy were never formally charged with murder or found guilty of any wrongdoing, it was revealed for the first time in January 2013 that a grand jury indicted both parents for the child's death in 1999. Charges were never filed because then District Attorney Alex Hunter refused to sign off on the indictment, perhaps because he knew the cross-finger pointing trick would stymie any effort to prove the charges beyond a reasonable doubt against either parent.

Let's play this out. Assume, hypothetically, that John Ramsey killed his daughter. One way for him to avoid being charged would be to make sure the evidence suggested that Patsy was involved, too. If, for example, he instructed Patsy to write the infamous ransom note, and forced her to help with the cover-up, John could easily demonstrate reasonable doubt by pointing at that evidence to imply that Patsy was the real killer. The murkier the evidence, the more effective the cross finger-pointing maneuver, and as the case unfolded, things became even murkier.

On the one hand, *Vanity Fair* published a story that said Patsy gave inconsistent statements about whether she found the ransom note before or after she noticed JonBenet missing from her bed. And former detective Steve Thomas wrote a book opining that Patsy Ramsey killed JonBenet because she was enraged about the child's bed-wetting.

On the other hand, investigators confronted John Ramsey at his lawyer's office about unusual Israeli black wool sweater fibers they discovered in the crotch area of the underwear JonBenet was wearing when her body was found. They told Ramsey the fibers matched one of his sweaters, but Ramsey refused to answer questions or explain how the fibers got there.

He might have argued that it was no big deal because he lived in the same house with his daughter, and the clothes might have landed in the same laundry basket. But the underpants were a size twelve (much too large for a six-year-old), and were taken from a brand new package that Patsy Ramsey had recently bought at Bloomingdales as a gift for JonBenet's older cousin.

After refusing to answer questions about the sweater fibers, Ramsey and his lawyer, Lin Wood, did what lawyers do when investigators back the suspect into a corner: They filibustered and used profanity. Ramsey said, "That's bullshit," and Wood fulminated about how he couldn't possibly answer questions without seeing the forensic report. Suffice it to say that if they had an innocent explanation at the time for such damning evidence, there would have been no yelling and no blather. If they have one now, I wish they would say so.

Despite the fiber evidence, if police believed John killed JonBenet, Patsy's seeming involvement would continue to frustrate prosecution efforts because of the very real risk that John could prevail at trial by pointing the finger at Patsy. Indeed, Patsy's red sweater fibers were found at the crime scene too - on duct tape that covered the child's mouth and intertwined in the ligature around the child's neck. It's not as damning as the black fibers in the underwear, but it suggests Patsy's contact with the child's body in the aftermath of her death, which is good enough if you're trying to muddy the water about who did what.

The cross-finger pointing trick is especially effective in a case like JonBenet Ramsey's where the public is uncomfortable believing that people who look kind and decent on the outside could be dastardly on the inside. This feel-good bias makes it hard for people, and by extension, jurors, to accept that a parent could commit a horrific crime against his or her own child, or that an innocent parent would help a killer-parent avoid prosecution. Even if prosecutors felt confident about the evidence, they had to worry about what the jurors would think.

After Patsy died of cancer in 2006, speculation was rampant that her death might lead to a break in the case. But in a cross-finger pointing situation, the death of one suspect changes nothing. The prosecutor still has to deal with the problem of the surviving suspect raising reasonable doubt by blaming the dead person. In a way, it's even better for the surviving suspect because it's even harder for prosecutors to rebut claims that the dead person did it if that person isn't around anymore to tell the truth.

To deal with this intensely frustrating dirty trick, we need police to treat all parental violence against children as highly vulnerable to the cross-finger pointing problem. This means always starting the investigation by immediately separating the parents and asking tough, even offensive, questions. Innocent parents won't mind, guilty ones will, and skilled detectives will be able to tell the difference.

We also need new ethical restraints that forbid defense attorneys to falsely point the finger of blame at an innocent person. It's one thing to claim that some unknown person is the real killer, but falsely accusing a real human being is wrong. These so-called Plan-B strategies not only pose a real risk that an innocent person may be wrongly convicted, they also incentivize criminals to drag innocent people into criminal activity to give them cover in the event they get caught. With increasing reports of criminals planting other people's DNA at crime scenes and doing other things to mess up the evidence, cross-finger pointing tactics are likely to become even more problematic in the future.

Another thing we can do is loosen ethical restrictions on prosecutors so they can continue with a case even if they aren't sure *beyond a reasonable doubt* that they can win a case against one suspect or the other in a cross-finger pointing situation. This should be the rule in circumstances where it can be established that the accused or his lawyer used a Plan-B suspect to inject false information into an investigation to prevent a prosecution.

Accused criminals deserve fair trials, but there is no Constitutional right to obstruct an investigation.

Cross-finger pointing tactics need to stop, especially if we want to do a better job prosecuting parental abuse of children and crimes where the people involved can use the private nature of family relationships to frustrate law enforcement efforts. That day will come a lot sooner if we start treating lawyers who use these vile tactics as accomplices to crime.

ELEVEN

Bullying the Advocates

People who speak up for victims in run-of-the-mill criminal cases get bullied all the time - usually by the bad guy or his buddies. High-profile trials are no different except that bullies get to use the media to help with the harassment; and they can balloon up the buddy pool with defense-attorney pundits and legal analysts to help with the dirty work.

I got a ton of bullying when I spoke up for the victims in the Scott Peterson, Kobe Bryant, and Michael Jackson cases. It comes with the territory but a few nuts acted like the cases were some sort of sick sporting event.

As with high stakes political contests, bullies in legal controversies come in two basic styles: professional and amateur. In the former category, you have defense attorneys and special-interest groups, like the ACLU. They wield astounding amounts of power in our society and have tremendous influence over public debates and judicial proceedings.

The amateurs tend to be like-minded people who form an ad hoc group to achieve a certain goal. (I don't mean amateur in a pejorative sense; I simply mean they're not formally organized as a business or political group, etc.)

When I step in to advocate for a victim in a high-profile case, the professional and amateur bullies kick into action, and I start getting emails and letters telling me to back down. In some cases, amateur trial-watchers send notes of support, but the bully mail comes in by the bushel; thank-you notes come in by ones and twos.

Frankly, neither the criticisms nor the compliments make a difference to me. I call cases like I see them no matter how unpopular my opinion might be, which is why I had no trouble predicting that Casey Anthony would be found not guilty of murdering her daughter Caylee. 99 percent of people who followed the case thought I was nuts, but I predicted two years before the trial started that Casey would be acquitted because the evidence showed that someone else killed the child. Casey was involved in nefarious activities, but she didn't kill Caylee. Whoever did wanted to punish Casey for something that happened in connection with those activities, something that made the killer very angry.

Good advocates know that public opinion isn't always right. We don't care if the victim or the perpetrator is beloved or reviled by the masses. Our job is to give voice to the voiceless and tell the truth. Other advocates who are not so good cave in to public pressure and support only certain types of victims, in certain kinds of cases. There will be more on this topic in chapter thirteen.

I wish I could say bullying never works to silence anyone because it shouldn't, but that's not always the case. When the intimidation gets intense and the people who support the perpetrator are especially powerful, some victim advocates cower and go silent.

When I'm tempted to go silent, I remind myself that when the bad guy is powerful, the person for whom I'm advocating doesn't usually have many allies, and more often than not, he or she has a multitude of newfound enemies. Whatever pressure I'm feeling either as an attorney for a victim or a pundit on television, the victim is feeling that pressure a hundred times over. Even when I'm getting threatened with lawsuits, I keep in mind that the victim may be getting death threats.

As a lawyer who fights for victims, it's my job to stay on task no matter the popularity of my position in the court of public opinion. Wouldn't you do the same for your client? What if the victim was your daughter, and you knew she was telling the truth, but everyone supported the perpetrator because he was a famous athlete? Would you stop supporting your child? Of course not.

Every crime victim is someone's child, no less deserving of our support, especially in the face of bully tactics.

Let me distinguish between "fighting" and "bullying." I love a good fight, and I respect skilled adversaries, even when I lose the debate. When both sides play by the rules, a good fight serves a purpose. Whether it's clarifying the key issues in a no-profile case or educating the public about legal principles in a high-profile case, most lawyers understand the power of healthy disagreement, and we certainly don't take it (or dish it) personally. That's why after I have a heated battle with a defense attorney on television, that attorney and I may wind up socializing after the show ends.

One of my fiercest combatants on the air, Jayne Weintraub, is a longtime personal friend. I've been to her home; she sent me a lovely baby gift when my last child was born; and we help each other with real-world cases. Yes, Jayne represents people who make my skin crawl, and I'm proud of her for that. But some defense lawyers are just vile. They start by intimidating the victims, then they move on to the advocates. I've developed many a migraine headache because of jerks who act less like legal professionals and more like the uncivilized clients they represent.

A few years ago, a lawyer on the other side of one of my high-profile cases filed an ethical complaint against me to stop me from talking to the media about a terrible injustice that had been perpetrated by him and his client. To nobody's great surprise, the complaint was dismissed as frivolous, and I responded by talking in public about the case even more. Eventually, I won a huge victory for my client, influenced in part by the public's outrage. It was also a victory for the justice system that a bottom-feeding jerk of a lawyer not only failed to muzzle me, but also caused even more of the truth to be told, because his attempt to squelch the facts generated even greater public interest in the real story. Bottom line: The bullies don't always win.

In a more recent case of bullying, John Ramsey's lawyer, Lin Wood, during an appearance on CNN's *Larry King Live*, repeatedly threatened to sue me for the opinions I expressed about the Ramsey case moments earlier on Paula Zahn's show. What the public didn't know was that right before Wood wasted all his airtime on Larry King's show talking about me, he called me personally to threaten me over the phone.

I knew ahead of time that Wood was a bully because his reputation for threatening people with lawsuits had preceded him. When I answered the phone, he sounded like he was making a well-rehearsed speech, rather than expressing earnest concern about his client's rights. "Wendy Murphy," he began, in a bombastic twang, "This is Lin Wood. I just heard you accuse my client of molesting and killing his daughter, and if I ever hear you say that again, you won't be ex-prosecutor Wendy Murphy, you'll be defendant Wendy Murphy in my lawsuit. Check my record!"

"Check your record?" I replied. "Kiss my a--!" I added a few more savory words, told him he had a lot of nerve threatening me, and suggested he take a flying leap. After I hung up, I smiled. Something I said hit a nerve.

What got Wood so riled up, you wonder? He heard me state my opinion that JonBenet Ramsey's death was related to child pornography. I explained that cops had executed several search warrants for child pornography on Ramsey's personal and professional computers. Police later said they found no pornography in the Ramsey *home*, but they have yet to reveal exactly what they *did* find on the various computers.

As I said on Paula Zahn's show, in the ugly world of child pornography, pictures of a young, fake-blonde (the Ramseys bleached the child's hair) gorgeous child are among the pictures most prized by perverts. Famed forensic medical examiner Dr. Cyril Wecht studied the autopsy report and opined in his book on the Ramsey case that JonBenet died accidentally from respiratory failure, and had significant vaginal injuries. He speculated that the use of a ligature around her neck may have been related to a sadistic sexual event.

As an expert in the field of sexual violence, I know that child pornography is a multibillion-dollar industry, and that, according to United States Attorney General Alberto Gonzalez, the most common producers of child porn are the victims' parents.

No, all of this doesn't mean the Ramseys are guilty, though a grand jury did vote to indict them in 1999, but it's certainly relevant and fair to talk about the evidence and debate potential theories about what happened.

The Ramseys themselves did exactly that when innocent men were being accused of the crime. It's interesting isn't it, that it's okay for them to discuss theories about innocent strangers being involved, but it's not okay for other people to discuss theories about the Ramseys' involvement.

As I explained on CNN right before Wood blew a gasket, claims about JonBenet being killed by a stranger were silly distractions because the autopsy findings showed evidence of both "acute" *and* "chronic" vaginal trauma. This means the child had new *and old* genital injuries. Those findings included epithelial erosion, chronic irritation and an eroded hymen that had been damaged to a point where only a small piece remained intact. Let me repeat, neither of the Ramseys was prosecuted, but it matters that if the person who killed JonBenet and caused her "acute" vaginal trauma is the same person who inflicted her *old* vaginal injuries, then the murderer had to be someone who had *ongoing* intimate access to the child.

It also matters that JonBenet had reportedly been to the pediatrician nearly thirty times between the ages of three and six. Several of those visits were for genital irritation and vaginal discomfort. Coincidence? Maybe. But child-abuse experts will tell you that mothers sometimes bring an abused child to a mandated reporter as a disguised cry for help, especially if she feels afraid or personally incapable of protecting her child from harm. The mandated reporter then takes responsibility for calling protective services to investigate.

After JonBenet's murder, the pediatrician said he saw no signs of abuse, though he never conducted an internal examination, so he wouldn't have seen the epithelial erosion or the eroded hymen.

The strange thing is, the Ramseys and their lawyers never seemed to care about the countless crazy theories that were being bandied about over the years. If they truly wanted to find the "real killer," they wouldn't have wanted nonsense about fake suspects making a bigger mess out of an already complicated case, and Lin Wood would have threatened to sue the people who were spewing nonsense instead of people who were trying to tell the truth about the evidence.

Who do you think benefits from this style of selective bullying? The public? The people trying to speak for JonBenet? The cops trying to do justice for an innocent child? Not a chance.

Nobody should be threatened with harm, financial or otherwise, for articulating an opinion about a matter of great public interest, such as the brutal murder of a defenseless child in her own home. But that's exactly what people like Lin Wood do when they don't like what someone is saying. And it's not unlike what fascist extremists do when they try to maintain political power and control over people by telling them all the horrible things that will happen if they don't speak and think a certain way, and obey the rules of the dictator.

Lin Wood claims to be driven by principle, but his principles must have been on vacation when he was representing the victim in the Kobe Bryant case. Wood was well aware of the false claim that his client had "sex with three men in three days" around the time of the incident; but he never went on CNN to threaten to sue anyone for making scandalous false statements about his already traumatized client.

If the victim had been my client, I would have at least filed ethical complaints against the defense lawyers, even lawsuits, if necessary, and I'd have gone on every talk show to tell the truth and denounce the lies. Lin Wood and his "principled" ilk did none of this.

I don't know why Lin Wood was reluctant to criticize Bryant's lawyers, and I don't much care, though it's interesting that the law firm that represented Bryant also represented the Ramseys, and Lin Wood presumably made plenty of money in both cases. The central point is that waffling on important principles is a sign that it isn't really about principles at all.

It is an abomination that lawyers can so profoundly disrespect the right to free speech, a core value from which all freedoms flow, by using the law and their authority as officers of the court to pound people into silence. Even speculative and offensive opinions have value in a legitimate search for the truth. As the United States Supreme Court has said many times, "The solution to offensive speech is more speech." This means that if Wood didn't like what I was saying, he should have debated me, not threatened me.

The public is entitled to know the truth about the Ramsey case, and more truth would be told if we could have full access to the files so we could intelligently discuss all the evidence. For example, what is the significance of the fact that the coroner found undigested pineapple in JonBenet's belly during the autopsy? We know she ate the fruit within approximately two hours of death and that when cops arrived, they found a bowl of pineapple on the kitchen table. The coroner estimated the child was killed around midnight, but the Ramseys told cops they brought JonBenet home sound asleep from a friend's Christmas party at about 9 p.m. and put her straight to bed without waking her.

John and Patsy adamantly denied giving the child pineapple, which makes a person wonder, what's so terrible about admitting that you gave your child pineapple?

Was the pineapple tested for the presence of drugs? If so, what were the results? And why did police spend so much time questioning the Ramseys about a seemingly innocuous bowl of fruit?

After aggressively insisting that neither he nor Patsy gave JonBenet pineapple on the night in question, why did John Ramsey feel the need to suggest that maybe JonBenet knew her killer, and they had a snack together before the murder?

Um - okay.

And why were the parents asked about prescription drugs in the home, specifically things like Klonopin, Xanax and Ativan? Drugs like these are not necessarily suspicious, but it's well known that they're sometimes used in child porn and sex abuse cases because they can cause amnesia, which makes it hard for the victims to recall what happened.

Benzodiazepines can be particularly dangerous for children, and can cause respiratory failure. Maybe the child died by accidental respiratory failure from the drugs. If the parents tried to revive the child by shaking her, that could explain reports that along with all the external injuries, JonBenet also suffered retinal damage consistent with shaking. It's time for the entire file to be released so we can know the whole truth, especially about why a grand jury concluded the Ramseys were responsible for JonBenet's death, but chose to indict them for "child abuse resulting in death" instead of murder.

Evidence also showed that there were attempts to stage the death as a brutal homicide by, for example, fracturing the child's skull (an injury described as post-mortem because it produced almost no blood). This made it especially difficult for the public to perceive the crime as anything but a vicious attack by a stranger. It's one thing to imagine parents accidentally killing a child, but ligatures around the neck and a fractured skull? No way.

Maybe the Ramseys needed the drugs for legitimate medical purposes, but then why would their lawyers allow them to answer so many probing personal questions about confidential medical information? Unless the topic of prescription drugs is relevant to a criminal investigation, questions about their use would be not only irrelevant but a violation of the Ramseys' constitutionally protected privacy rights.

If I represented a suspect and police wanted to ask questions about my client's use of Viagra, for example, I would object and instruct my client not to answer if I thought the question had nothing to do with the case. Maybe cops wanted to know whether the Ramseys were sedated on the night in question - which would explain why they didn't hear any noises. But if that was the purpose of the questions, wouldn't police have simply said, "Did you take any prescription drugs or other sleep aids before bedtime?" and if the Ramseys said, "No," just leave it at that?

Reasonable people have long wanted to know more about why cops asked about the drugs, and what tests were done on the bowl of pineapple. Full disclosure of the case file would give us the answers but most of the investigation is still under wraps after more than fifteen years,

The file might also explain that weird one-night private plane trip to Michigan that John Ramsey had scheduled for December 26th, the day after JonBenet died. The Ramseys told police it was a prescheduled trip to their summer home on one of the Great Lakes in northern Michigan. They said the whole family was meeting up with John's two adult children from a previous marriage and that they were getting together to celebrate Christmas. Sounds lovely, right? But who takes a tiny plane from Colorado to a summer home at the Canadian border in the middle of winter for a one-night stay?

The flight would have taken about five hours (they reportedly had to stop along the way and pick up John's adult children) which means they would have landed in Michigan on the afternoon of Thursday the 26th - only to have to turn around the next day and head back to Boulder on that same long flight because John, Patsy, Burke and JonBenet had commercial airline tickets to Florida, out of Denver, on Saturday morning, the 28th. The Ramseys were curiously unclear about these dates when asked about the purported Christmas trip to Michigan. They told police they had no clothes packed for the trip, and John said the only thing he was planning to bring was his laptop. Does that make sense? I'm not saying it's not possible the Ramseys were planning a Norman Rockwell moment, but such a long flight in an overcrowded tiny plane for a one-night Christmas visit to a summer home at the Canadian border in the dead of winter? I think there's more to that story and the public has a right not only to ask questions about it, but also to expect answers.

It's been reported that only 10 percent of the evidence in the case has been revealed thus far, even though under public records laws, the entire file is supposed to be released after a decision is made not to file charges. An exception to the law allows officials to keep things under wraps so long as an investigation is "ongoing." When it's a murder case, the file could theoretically be "ongoing" forever because there is no statute of limitations on murder. But judges typically give prosecutors only a decade or so to solve the crime before releasing the file to the public. If a major development in the case occurs before the ten years is up, officials can argue that they need another ten years to investigate the new leads.

Thinking about public records laws made me wonder whether the "bombshell" news a few years ago about a man named John Mark Karr confessing to the crime would conveniently keep the file secret for another ten years under the theory that Karr was a "new" lead in the case. It didn't go unnoticed that Karr popped up out of nowhere right around the ten year mark.

As it quickly turned out, Karr had nothing to do with the child's death, and was nowhere near Boulder, Colorado when JonBenet died, which begs the question: Why was his charade indulged by then District Attorney Mary Lacey? (Seriously, did voters ever check her IQ?) Karr's arrest created more confusion about the case and erected yet another barrier to full disclosure of the truth.

I hope the public never loses interest in the case, not because the death of JonBenet Ramsey is more important than the death of any other child, but because the public's understanding of what really happened in a high-profile case influences how we feel when we hear similar stories.

Cable news shows are full of lawyers who will stop at nothing to bludgeon a search for the truth. In the particular mini-drama of the Ramsey case, the good news is that people noticed how Wood overreacted to my comments on Paula Zahn's show, which not only made people even more suspicious of whether Wood was telling the truth, it also created its own little news story. Far from a successful silencing ploy, Wood's bluster and threats afforded me the chance to appear on even more programs where I talked even more about the case and the evidence.

The press sometimes shines a light on the truth, but too often, it indulges bullies by allowing defense attorneys to smack people around while everyone else has to play nice in the sandbox.

TWELVE

Selling Unfair Punishment as "Restorative Justice"

One of the strangest and most radical criminal-loving propositions to gain momentum in the criminal justice system is an idea called restorative justice. It's creeping its evil way into courtrooms across America and very few people are paying attention.

It's evil in part because it sounds so humane, fair and effective. After all: What could possibly be wrong with *restoring* a person in the name of justice? The unpleasant truth, though, is that this warped philosophy allows the most dangerous criminals to be released from prison early, or never locked up at all, so long as they make nice with their victims. The charade begins with officials trying to persuade victims that punishment serves no legitimate purpose, and that the victim will feel better if the perpetrator apologizes. In exchange for the apology, the criminal gets to walk free. If it weren't such a dangerous idea, I'd laugh out loud.

Remember Edward Cashman, the Vermont judge I told you about in the introduction who sentenced a repeat child rapist to only sixty days in prison? It turns out Cashman taught and promoted the theory of restorative justice to law students in his spare time, something the public learned about only after the judge found himself in the middle of a firestorm of public criticism. And it only got worse for Cashman when he tried to justify the ridiculously lenient sentence by invoking a core tenet of restorative justice philosophy: He said that harsh punishment and a lengthy prison sentence would accomplish nothing.

Whoa! Hold on, judge!

Since when is public safety nothing? With judges like Cashman on the bench, is it any wonder that while the crime rate overall is fairly low in Vermont, sex crimes were up by over 60 percent in 2004, compared to the number of offenses in 2003? This is what Vermonters get in exchange for judges who promote restorative justice. I'm sure they're grateful.

There is no uniformly accepted definition of restorative justice, and to the extent it is being used in some states to the benefit of victims without a quid pro quo discount in punishment to criminals, I have no objection. But the fundamental premise of this nutty idea in most places is that punishment should be de-emphasized and prosecution avoided in favor of a negotiated non-punitive plea deal. To facilitate this, the judge allows the criminal to barter against the psychological and financial needs of victims by apologizing and paying the victim some trivial sum to make the case go away.

Let me sharpen that up a little bit. Restorative justice is an approach that allows perpetrators to trade the value of an apology and a few bucks in return for the victim's acceptance of a wrist-slap, which in many cases translates into the outright dismissal of serious felony charges.

This is silliness. A perpetrator should be punished, *and* he should apologize, *and* he should pay the victim money after she files a civil suit when the criminal case is over. These things are not mutually exclusive. In fact, they are intimately and productively related.

And let's get real: If a criminal apologizes because he thinks it's going to get him a discount on his sentence, it isn't much of an apology anyway. So there's very little real restoration going on.

The sad fact is that many victims are more than happy to take any offer to avoid a stressful criminal trial, and defense attorneys have a vested interest in keeping strong prosecution witnesses off the witness stand. But victims are entitled to know the truth about what's really going on; and the truth is that restorative justice is far more beneficial to the bad guy than to the victim; and it does absolutely nothing for society at large.

Do you think Cashman is a rare example of this idea? He isn't. Judges like Cashman are promoting restorative justice in courtrooms all across the country, despite the fact that punishment is an appropriate and effective response to crime.

Serious violence should never be minimized, especially when we're talking about things like child sex abuse, which is very difficult to uncover because kids are so easy to silence. For the most part, children can't protect themselves from adults, and the people who violate children are extraordinarily skilled at terrorizing their victims to make sure they don't tell. When judges do have a chance to punish one of these monsters, they have to take the opportunity to send the strongest possible message of intolerance. The judge has to say, "You are going to prison for a very long time because sexual abuse of children is a very serious crime. There are no second bites at the apple. You will never hurt another child ever again. Period."

Restorative justice sends the opposite message: "Child sex abuse isn't so bad. You are not going to prison because, although the child will suffer emotional harm for the rest of her life, she doesn't have any broken bones. I'll give you another chance because you told the victim you were sorry, and you gave her some money, so everyone has been restored. Let's adjourn the court proceedings, and gather around the tree in front of the courthouse for a rousing rendition of Kumbaya."

When a child predator hears this type of message, he walks away laughing at the foolishness of anyone who thinks he'll never touch another child again. All the guy is thinking about is how glad he is that he didn't have to go to prison, where the population of potential new victims is zero. Child predators are among the most cunning of all criminals; yet judges like Edward Cashman feed their pathology by touting the power of an apology and a hug. That's like handing a homeless alcoholic five bucks, but only after he promises to spend it on milk and cookies. Give me a break.

I'm not saying punishment is the only thing that matters or that the system doesn't need more and better treatment for all prisoners. And it would be great if we could get more rapists and killers to accept responsibility for their crimes - an aspect of restorative justice that I support. But we can't let the criminal justice system become a marketplace, in which negotiations for reductions in punishments are treated like real estate deals. I'll say it again: Justice should be better than capitalism.

To appreciate how ridiculous the concept of restorative justice really is, it's important to remember that "criminal justice" is not just a phrase attached to the process by which we grind out convictions and stash the guilty people behind bars. It means truth and fairness in the redress of serious public wrongdoing, and it is a core concept around which our society is organized. Justice is a philosophical backbone from which we draw inspiration about the value of humanity and derive direction about how to treat one another with civility and respect. This means that how we do justice is both a message sender and a mirror on our collective beliefs. What do we think is valuable enough to be worthy of meaningful protection, and are we conveying a clear message about those values in the way crimes are being punished? When the justice system fails to reflect society's values in the way it deals with crime, civility suffers and respect for law itself suffers. The only one who doesn't suffer is the criminal. How is this good for society, or fair, or wise?

Restorative justice types are right about at least one thing: The system is broken. But it isn't broken in a way that requires us to go easy on criminals. On the contrary, the system is broken because criminals and their lawyers have had the courts by the throat for far too long. We don't need more coddling of the bad guys. We need reforms that give back some measure of legitimacy to a system that has had people in other nations laughing at us ever since the O.J. Simpson case, even as we boast about our superiority.

Restorative justice literally decriminalizes violence by reducing the personal costs criminals are expected to endure as payment for their crimes. It doesn't take much deep reflection to see how making crimes cheaper to commit makes them easier to commit. Nor is it hard to see how minimizing punishment will reduce the value of human life by rendering the power of law impotent to promote the essential value of mutual respect in society.

Certain kinds of crimes, especially sex crimes against children, are so out of control in this country, we desperately need the exact opposite of what restorative justice offers. I might feel differently if scientifically valid data proved that restorative justice reduced crime in some significant way, but there is simply no good evidence that it does anything at all to prevent violence.

Take juvenile offenders, for example. We tried a restorative approach for a long time and it didn't work. Reasonable people argued that when it comes to kids who commit crimes, we should try creative, non-punitive alternatives to incarceration. After all, kids are less morally culpable than adults, and they are certainly more fixable.

Their brains aren't even done growing, which means maybe we can still make a difference if we get involved early in the lives of troubled kids, and get them on track to achieve an education and become invested in their futures, etc. It all sounds lovely, but for the most part, it doesn't work. I'm not saying no child can be saved, but as a policy matter, the numbers just aren't there to justify a wholly soft-on-crime approach for criminals - no matter their age.

During the 1970s and '80s, the criminal justice system was deeply committed to a purely rehabilitative approach to juvenile crime. Even kids who committed murder rarely suffered any real punishment or incarceration. They went into treatment and social service programs, and we spent a fortune trying to repair the mental software of young people who were getting into trouble with the law.

In the aftermath of this period, kids began committing more serious crimes at younger ages than ever before. One reasonable interpretation of this data is that kids got the message that they could commit virtually any crime with impunity. Rob a store - get a hug. Kill a person - go to therapy. No wonder things got worse.

Some claim the rehabilitation model wasn't a complete failure because juvenile crime rates went down overall, although it's likely that demographic shifts explain that data. The main point is that juveniles today are more violent at younger ages than ever before, and this directly follows a period in which the juvenile justice system was primarily restorative, rather than punishment oriented.

With this experience just behind us and with states having responded across the board with new, tougher laws to deal with juvenile offenders, it is shocking to see otherwise smart people promoting restorative ideas for adult criminals. If it didn't work for kids, why in the world would it work for adults? The public's growing outrage over leniency for violent offenders is strong evidence that society is literally on the verge of becoming violent about the idea of restorative justice. Just look at what happened when the Judge Cashman story broke.

Led by Bill O'Reilly on the Fox News Channel, protests of Cashman's decision emerged across the country overnight. People of all political stripes and persuasions were incredulous. Cashman tried to cover for his inane decision by suggesting he only gave Hulett sixty days behind bars because he wanted the defendant to get treatment, and treatment was only available to certain high-level offenders in prison. Low-level offenders had to wait to get help until they were released from prison, he claimed, and Hulett was deemed a low-level offender.

Let's not get hung up on the absurdity of calling Hulett a low-level offender, although that certainly deserves some scrutiny. A fair number of people took comfort from the fact that Cashman had an explanation for the sixty-day sentence. But that comfort didn't last long as it was soon revealed that Cashman's explanation was untrue. Cashman had agreed with the defense attorney to a sentence of no more than 90 days long before it was determined whether Hulett would be deemed a low-risk or high-risk offender. In other words, Cashman agreed to a trivial jail term long before he knew whether Hulett would be eligible for treatment in prison.

It's bad enough when a judge cuts some serious slack for a confessed child rapist, but then to lie about it? I could almost respect the guy if he stuck to his guns and said, "Look, I think prison is bad for people, and I'm willing to take the heat for my ideological bias," or something like that. But he didn't have the guts to stand up for his convictions. Instead, he spun like a madman and made up a story about wanting to help a vicious sex offender get treatment. The worst part is: Many people in Vermont bought it.

Several newspapers made Cashman out to be some kind of folk hero, touting the judge for using the Hulett case to pressure the prison system to make treatment available to all levels of sex criminals. The Vermont Press Association even gave the guy a First Amendment award in the fall of 2006 for his commitment to "openness in government." Seriously! When I first heard about the award, I thought it was a joke. Shouldn't an award in the name of the First Amendment be saved for government officials who at least tell the truth about how they conduct the people's business?

This kind of silliness fuels the idea that the media has a liberal anti-prosecution bias. I can understand that the fourth estate is supposed to provide a check against unfair government power. But what about holding the government accountable when it systematically *fails to use* its power to protect defenseless children?

After 9/11, liberal media outlets supported prosecutions and harsh punishments for hate-motivated violence against innocent Muslims living in the United States. This helped to hold judges and prosecutors accountable for responsible enforcement of hate crimes laws, which, in turn, helped deter violence against Muslims. What I want to know is, how come the media doesn't see itself as having a similar responsibility to watch over the government's inertia when it comes to other forms of targeted violence—especially against powerless children?

In my opinion, the award wasn't so much a prize for Cashman as a punishment for Bill O'Reilly. The Vermont media knew that O'Reilly had exposed a terrible injustice and brought well-deserved shame to bear on the whole state. Many good people there were mortified by Cashman's conduct, but many in power were cheering the idea that a judge refused to incarcerate a dangerous criminal, and they were furious with O'Reilly. So the press gave Cashman a prize.

A similar thing happened to me after I exposed a Massachusetts judge who tried to help convicted rapist James Kelly stay out of prison. I exposed Judge Dan Toomey for perpetuating Kelly's fraud and *Massachusetts Lawyers'*

Weekly (a notoriously pro-defense publication) responded by giving Toomey an award. I'd worked with Judge Toomey in the past, so I went to the award ceremony because I wanted him to know that even though he'd been embarrassed in my case, I still remembered all the good things he'd done in other cases. It was weird, though, watching a judge get accolades for bad behavior.

I wouldn't have minded so much if Cashman or Toomey legitimately wanted to help criminals reform their lives. My brother's childhood friend got involved with drugs as a young man, and his addiction led to repeated incarcerations - mostly for driving under the influence of drugs. His wife breathed a sigh of relief when he got locked up because she knew he would at least be safe for a while. After he wrapped up a sentence, he'd stay sober for a time; but the addiction was powerful, and he'd get into trouble repeatedly. The last time he got out, he told his wife he'd stay clean forever. He had two little kids, and he knew his addiction was hurting them. But he didn't last long before dying from an overdose. Everyone who knew him said he might have had a chance if there had been treatment available in prison and good follow-up care on the outside. We'll never know.

So sympathy for criminals isn't ridiculous, but Cashman stepped way over the line from sympathy to lunacy, and the protests against him became so intense that Cashman was forced to increase Hulett's sentence from sixty days to three years, but it was too little too late. The harsh criticism of Cashman continued, and he eventually resigned from the bench in the fall of 2006.

I had already been working with Bill O'Reilly for a while when all of this transpired. He had hired me to help promote Florida's Jessica Lunsford Act – a law named for a child who'd been sexually abused and murdered by a convicted sex offender who should have been behind bars.

Jessica's Law requires mandatory long-term incarceration of child molesters, and GPS tracking devices for life. Bill wanted to get Jessica's Law passed in all fifty states and he covered the Cashman story to illustrate why the law is a good idea.

Bill's extensive coverage of the Cashman situation was a watershed moment in the American criminal justice system because no judge had ever before *increased* a criminal's punishment in response to public outcry.

I had seen plenty of cases where public pressure made a judge *reduce* someone's punishment, but not increase it. Take, for example, the prosecution of Louise Woodward, the killer-nanny I wrote about in chapter eight. Massachusetts Judge Hiller Zobel allowed Woodward to walk free the very day she was convicted of murder, in part because large crowds of Woodward supporters had gathered outside the courthouse over the course of the multi-week trial.

Some of the protesters were reportedly paid to be there, while others showed up for the television cameras. Whatever the motivation of the protesters, pressure outside the courthouse produced benefits for Woodward inside the courthouse. Judge Zobel was well aware of the crowds when he reduced Woodward's conviction from murder to manslaughter and sentenced the baby-killer to time served. The judge sent Woodward home instead of to prison where she belonged.

Turning up the heat to help criminals go free is nothing new, but before O'Reilly took on Cashman, no one had ever successfully lobbied for an *increase* in punishment. Besides being a huge victory for O'Reilly, it was an important message to our legal system. The restorative justice stuff had exploded in Cashman's face, and people were taking to the streets. I got tons of e-mails from people who were furious about the Cashman situation. Some talked about vigilantism; most were just venting. I always discourage people from taking the law into their own hands, but when people start talking about vigilante justice, it's an important sign that the law is not working as it should.

The public is now on full alert that there are judges like Cashman all across the country, quietly doling out lenient sentences to dangerous criminals. Some do not mention restorative justice, but their decisions reflect an ideology that favors leniency over fairness and public safety.

Pennsylvania Judge Rayford A. Means was chastised by his own appellate court in 2006 for being too lenient with a sex offender named Tracy McIntosh. Means sentenced the guy to house arrest even after he was presented with unequivocal evidence that McIntosh was a vicious sex offender. Means said the rape was "bad judgment," "inappropriate," and "dishonorable behavior," not unlike getting drunk in public. Someone should have told Judge Means that, according to the United States Supreme Court, rape is the ultimate violation of a human being, short of murder.

Thanks to the integrity of the Pennsylvania appellate courts, McIntosh's sentence of house arrest was overturned, and Judge Means got a good tongue-lashing for trying to excuse his weak sentence in terminology suggestive of a restorative justice agenda. Means actually said to the convicted rapist: "I do not believe you have to be warehoused. I think you just have to be directed in the right direction." The appellate court laudably wrote that the punishment did not "fit the crime," and that Judge Means gave "far too much weight" to McIntosh's "rehabilitative needs" compared to the needs of society and the harm to the victim.

There are many more judges like Cashman and Means out there - too many to include in this chapter - so it's important to pay attention when judges refuse to punish offenders with sentences proportionate to the crime. When you come across such a judge, do something about it. No, we can't stop judges from believing in crazy ideas, but we can all play a role in making sure they don't act on their personal beliefs.

And let's have a civilized discussion with proponents of restorative justice to see if there's any common ground. For example, they believe offenders should take responsibility for their crimes, which is a good thing, and they cite the old Native American justice system as an example of a culture that prevented violence by relying on shame and stigma rather than incarceration. We should point out to proponents of restorative justice that if they really believe in the power of stigma, they should support sex-offender registries. And if they really believe Native Americans had it right, they should support long-term mandatory punishment for child rapists because Native Americans banished those guys from the tribe. One strike, and they were gone. No feather passing to child predators.

With Jessica's Law in place in every state, judges would have no fudge room when punishing child predators. Mandatory prison sentences would be imposed on all child predators, and the rate of sex crimes against kids would drop overnight.

While we're waiting for all fifty states to get on board, we need laws that require judges to issue annual report cards, in which they reveal the sentences they give out in child sex abuse cases. Report card laws like the ones in place in Virginia and Pennsylvania allow the public to see whether certain judges are more likely than others to give unjust discounts to certain types of criminals. Judges who care about protecting kids will welcome this form of public oversight.

Finally, we need better judicial accountability. Mothers Against Drunk Driving is a good example of how a citizens' group can make a difference. Through court-watch programs, publicity campaigns, and political activism, MADD has been extremely effective at holding judges accountable in drunk-driving cases. Now we need parents to do the same thing for child sex crimes. I even have a good idea for the name of the group: Mothers And Fathers Incensed Over Sex Offenders, or MAFIOSO.

MAFIOSO has a nice, ominous ring to it, doesn't it? Makes it sound like the members mean business. I know I do. Do you?

THIRTEEN

Co-opting the Public with the Victims' Rights Charade

Most of you have heard something about victims' rights, even if you've never been involved in a criminal case. But did you know that despite reams of victims' rights laws on the law books in every state in this country, these laws are almost never enforced?

Most victims are never even told they have rights, much less what they should do about it if their rights are threatened or violated. It's worse than that, really. Victims' rights laws are mostly toothless tigers. They look good on paper but rarely help victims achieve justice.

These laws say nice things like, "The victim has the right to be treated with dignity and respect." Well, okay, but I've never seen a judge order anyone to respect a victim or restore a victim's dignity. Even when a perpetrator harasses a victim and her family, or when a defense attorney gratuitously insults a victim during trial or violates her privacy by asking irrelevant questions about her personal life, the judge never says a word about how these things violate the victim's right to be treated with "dignity and respect."

One of the most common victims' rights laws promises victims a speedy trial. Some states call it a right to a "prompt disposition." The name really doesn't matter because the point is that victims need and deserve to have their cases resolved swiftly, but often their interests are ignored in favor of criminals who want their trials to be delayed until all the witnesses drop dead.

If victims' rights laws had any value at all, a victim could stand up in court and ask the judge to speed up the trial, or at least put a stop to all the strategic delay tactics. But in most states, victims stay silent because the laws contain a sneaky clause stuck somewhere toward the end that says something like "none of the aforementioned rights shall be enforceable."

Think about that. Lawmakers passed a law to help victims, and made it unenforceable. What's the point? Imagine the outrage if a "no enforcement clause" had been added to the law that gave women the right to vote. The obvious message would be: Sure you can vote - just don't actually show up on election day because we might not let you in, and there's nothing you can do about it.

A law with no teeth is worse than no law at all because it's patronizing and because it sets in stone the idea that victims are not worthy of *real* rights. It truly is the ultimate in dirty tricks when lawmakers - often defense lawyers in states like Massachusetts - dupe people into believing they just passed a terrific new bill when in reality they just dealt victims a colossal insult.

Not every law can or should be equally enforceable. Let's face it: Even though the pursuit of happiness is in the Declaration of Independence, you can't exactly march into court and file a lawsuit when you're not feeling chipper. But it is downright un-American to co-opt people into silence by making them think they have rights when they really have nothing but nice-sounding legal mumbo-jumbo.

If victims' rights were enforceable, as they should be, it would never have taken more than three years for Robert Blake's case to come to trial because the judge would have respected the victim's speedy trial rights. (Yes, even homicide victims have rights; they belong to surviving family members.)

If victims' rights were enforceable, Rhode Island Judge Francis Darigan could never have agreed to a plea deal in 2006 for the owners of a nightclub whose use of dangerous insulation led to the deaths of a hundred people in a tragic fire. The judge gave the owners a deal (one got no prison time at all) *without* first hearing from the victims' families about the impact of the crime on their lives, even though the law requires that victims be allowed to make an impact statement *before* punishment is determined.

If victims' rights were enforceable, the lawyer for convicted kidnapper Stephen Fagan never could have gotten away with disrespecting the victim during Fagan's sentencing hearing after his 1999 conviction. Fagan kidnapped his two young daughters from their mother in Massachusetts when they were very young, then fled to Florida and changed their names. When the girls were found some twenty years later, Fagan was remarried to a wealthy woman. After his arrest, Fagan hired an expensive attorney and a PR firm. Public criticism of the girls' mother soon followed. She was vilified for allegedly *causing* Fagan to kidnap the children by being a bad mother. It was heart wrenching to see the near-daily torturing of a woman whose life had already been ruined by the loss of her children. Even the children, by this time young women, didn't seem to care about their mother's feelings, though it's easy to understand why. They'd been living with their kidnapper for years. Who knows what they were told about why their mother wasn't around.

It was hard for the public to feel sympathy for a mom whose kidnapped children weren't posing for joyous reunion photo-ops.

A normal defense attorney would have appreciated that the children sided with his client and just shut his mouth about the girls' mother. After all, Fagan had no defense. If bad parenting were a legitimate defense to kidnapping, someone would have snatched O.J. Simpson's kids a long time ago.

The judge ruled that Fagan could not argue that his wife's problems justified the kidnapping, which meant that all the talk about the mother's issues years earlier (even assuming it was true, and much of it was not) was completely irrelevant. But that didn't stop Fagan's defense attorney from trashing the woman while the case was being litigated.

With public sentiment being manipulated by the defense with the help of a PR agency, hatred for the mother and sympathy for the kidnapper rose to such a level that Fagan's attorney, Richard Egbert, was able to pressure the prosecutor to offer a plea bargain. Fagan would plead guilty but would only pay a fine and be placed on probation. After the deal was struck, the lawyers went to court to have the sentence imposed. That's when things got really ugly.

With the national news media in the courtroom, Egbert's sadistic ego took over. Rather than accepting the deal quietly, he made a wild-eyed speech about how the girls' mother had psychological and other irrelevant personal problems. Remember, the judge had already ruled that whatever problems the mother had when the girls were young, they were irrelevant to the crime of kidnapping. Period.

This was a relatively simple case of a guilty kidnapper getting a great deal from a judge, so you'd think Egbert would have just taken the gift and gotten out of there with his client fast, right? Wrong. Egbert went on and on about the mother's past with television cameras playing the ugly sideshow live in front of the whole country. She sat there, silent and dignified, while he spewed venom about her, for no purpose, in front of millions of people. The fact that Egbert's client had ruined this woman's life decades earlier wasn't bad enough; Egbert opened up that wound, grabbed a pile of salt, and rubbed it right in.

This is a perfect example of how victims' rights laws have no value. If they were enforceable, a lawyer for the mother could have jumped up and objected. If victims had a *real* right to be treated with dignity, or even a way of asking the judge to stop defense attorneys from violating their privacy rights, someone could have stopped Egbert before he opened his mouth. Everyone knew that what Egbert was saying was deeply personal, largely false *and* had been ruled irrelevant. But because victims' rights laws are unenforceable, nobody did anything.

When victims try to complain about their rights being violated, judges tell them they have no "standing" to be heard. "You're not a party to the case," they say. But just because a victim isn't a party doesn't mean she shouldn't be allowed to speak, or that a judge shouldn't care. Too many judges don't pay attention to victims' rights because they know they aren't enforceable.

This is why lawyers who care about victims are fighting to get rid of unenforceability clauses, and it's why I spend even more time teaching victims about *other* rights that *are* enforceable and that have nothing to do with "victims' rights" statutes.

I'm talking about Constitutional rights like privacy and due process; rights that are threatened every time a defense attorney says something out loud about a victim's personal troubles, or seeks access to a victim's medical and counseling files. To protect these interests, I came up with an idea called "Privacy Miranda Rights," which involves teaching victims that they have the right to say, "None of your damn business," when defense attorneys, cops, prosecutors or investigators ask probing, irrelevant questions about their personal lives in connection with a criminal case. If accused criminals can be empowered by regular Miranda laws to refuse to answer *all* questions during an investigation, then innocent citizens should be authorized to resist *unfair* questions.

Naysayers criticize lawyers who work for victims by suggesting we're motivated by the possibility of winning a big civil suit after the criminal trial is over, and sometimes this is true. But many victims' lawyers help victims for no financial reward. For example, scores of attorneys from the American Trial Lawyers Association donated countless hours of legal services to the victims of 9/11 and their families. These lawyers knew victims' families would need compensation as quickly as possible so they could pay the rent, buy food, and obtain desperately needed medical and psychological care. While the lawyers could have charged a fee, every one of them worked for nothing - to the tune of many millions of dollars. Few people even know about this story because the lawyers who donated their time also refused to accept recognition for their generosity.

Unfortunately, this noble approach to lawyering is harder to find when it comes to helping victims in run-of-the-mill criminal cases. Some of us do a lot of pro bono work, but most attorneys who claim to be "victims' rights" lawyers only show up when there's a camera around or when there's much money to be made. Even lawyers who usually represent criminals will come out of the woodwork and claim to be "victims' rights" lawyers when there's money to be made.

Criminal attorney Joe Tacopina from New York, for example, routinely insults crime victims and shills for the defense as a pundit on cable news shows. But when he was offered the chance to make a ton of money representing the family of Imette St. Guillen, a young woman who was brutally raped and murdered by a bouncer at a New York bar in 2006, Tacopina was only too happy to change his tune and start singing the woes of crime victims. It would be interesting to know how much he got paid when the case settled, so we can all know the price of a defense attorney's soul.

Victims and their families are free to hire whomever they want. There's certainly nothing illegal or unethical about Tacopina representing crime victims no matter how much he insults them on television. But it would sure help the good guys if victims and their families did a little research before hiring a "victims' rights" lawyer. If a victim hires a lawyer whose firm makes a living representing criminals or insurance companies, the money that lawyer makes from the civil suit will be used in other cases to undermine the rights and interests of victims. Alternatively, if victims' families hire a lawyer who refuses to represent criminals and insurance companies, the lawyer's fees are far more likely be used to improve the legal system on behalf of all victims.

Some of the settlement money that goes to lawyers sincerely dedicated to advocacy for victims is also likely to land in the pockets of organizations like the Ally Foundation; a nonprofit foundation that works tirelessly to reform sex offender laws to better protect public safety.

Other worthy organizations include the It Happened to Alexa Foundation, which gives money to crime victims so they can pay for travel and lodging expenses associated with their participation in criminal trials; the Domestic Violence Registry, which provides the public with free 24/7 access to a national database of information about violent perpetrators; Protect.org, which works with legislatures around the country to repair arcane laws, such as overly tight statutes of limitation; Bikers Against Child Abuse (bacausa.org), which does countless things to promote child safety, including literally showing up on motorcycles to physically protect endangered children; Justice for Children which helps protective parents fight for justice in family court; Children Without A Voice, which bravely speaks up for kids when nobody else will; and the Maryland Crime Victims' Resource Center, which provides excellent information and services to support crime victims and their families.

The Women's and Children's Advocacy Project at New England Law I Boston, a program I co-direct at my law school's Center for Law and Social Responsibility, provides volunteer legal services to help all these groups when they need us. My students write cutting edge legal briefs and work on many interdisciplinary projects to advance the rights of victimized women and children and improve their access to justice.

All these organizations would fare better if victims' civil cases were referred *only* to lawyers with a demonstrated record of prioritizing the rights of victims. I'm talking about lawyers who not only have much experience, but also do a lot of pro bono work for victims and *refuse* to represent criminals and insurance companies

Keep in mind that some people who claim to be advocates for victims may actually be working to undermine their rights. For example, rape crisis centers and child advocates in Vermont were either silent about or supportive of the Judge Cashman situation. What's that about?

Advocates who don't believe criminals should receive just punishments for their crimes should be doing different work, if for no other reason than because studies show that crime rates go down as prosecution rates go up. Some liberals oppose the very idea of prosecution and say it's oppressive. But these people see enforcement of hate crimes laws as liberating. How can some prosecutions be oppressive while others are liberating? And isn't it just common sense that widespread sexual violence is more harmful to the freedom of women and children than anything the government is doing to take away the freedom of child predators?

There is good news to report. Dissension is growing in the ranks of left-leaning victim advocacy groups, mainly because their soft-on-crime approach hasn't worked and people who *really* care about victims are fed up. After more than thirty years of relatively ineffective "advocacy," new leaders are emerging, and they're talking about improving prosecution rates as a way of *preventing* violence.

Advocates who want to see more prosecutions deserve much credit for going against the ideological grain, especially considering that if more prosecutions lead to a reduction in sexual violence rates, some advocates will lose their jobs, as well they should, because we won't have as many victims!

In the meantime, we need more lawyers getting on board to help victims quickly after the crime happens. Lawyers should be accompanying victims to police stations to ensure that cops ask only fair and relevant questions, just as criminal lawyers often accompany their clients to police stations to protect the rights of the accused. And victim lawyers should be present in the courtroom as often as necessary, to make sure the victim's personal rights and interests are protected.

Believe me, it will make a big difference just to have a lawyer in the room because prosecutors, judges and defense lawyers who are even *thinking* about pulling a stunt, or violating a victim's rights, will think twice if they know the victim's attorney is watching their every move.

FOURTEEN

Claiming a Suspect Passed a Polygraph

Defense attorneys love to make noisy announcements about how their clients passed polygraph tests. For most of us, this conjures up images of hard-nosed detectives hooking up a lie detector in the station house under a single, unshaded bulb hanging from the ceiling, and practically daring the subject to tell even the smallest white lie. We put much of stock in claims about polygraphs because we assume they measure the truth. Who could possibly stay cool enough not to be proved a liar in such intimidating circumstances?

Even though polygraph exams are not admissible in most courts, police and criminals alike know that a well-done test is very valuable during the investigative phase because it can reveal whether a suspect is being truthful. This is why cops often ask a suspect whether he is willing to submit to a lie detector. If he says, "Absolutely, right now," police usually look elsewhere for the real criminal. But if he says, "Maybe," or, "Okay, but in a few days," or, "I would but my lawyer advised me not to," then you know you're looking at a guy who's probably guilty as sin. And if the guy does sit for a police-administered polygraph, and he passes, you're probably looking at an innocent man.

There are no absolutes with lie detector machines, which makes sense because they don't really measure truth anyway. They measure heart rate, sweat, and physiological responses to questions - but not truth. So we shouldn't think of these machines as having slam-dunk power one way or the other.

But we should be extra suspicious when the suspect paid an "expert" to conduct the test. Law enforcement officials everywhere will tell you that while polygraphs are not perfect, there are far more false negatives (guilty people passing the test) than there are false positives (innocent people failing them). And tests performed by cops are much more reliable than tests performed by suspects' hired guns because law enforcement polygraphs are subjected to all kinds of rules and restrictions, while defense attorneys are under no obligation to conduct polygraphs under any specified conditions. The lack of any standard oversight when suspects submit to their own polygraph testing makes defense claims about suspects "passing" the tests utterly meaningless. This is why you don't hear defense attorneys talk much about the test conditions. They talk about the credentials of the "expert" who administered the test and his years of experience, blah blah blah, but they don't tell you what the "expert" did to mess with the integrity of the test to produce a false result.

The point is, it doesn't matter *who* conducted the test if the examiner didn't set up the right conditions, first. According to longtime polygrapher Jack Nasuti, nothing can be determined about the results of a polygraph examination without knowing details about the calibration and quality of the machine, test preparation (including the suspect's pretest interview), the condition of the person being examined, the types of questions asked, and, perhaps most important of all, whether the suspect took steps to fake the results through the ingestion of drugs or other substances, or by learning how to trick the machine with techniques widely available on the Internet.

Remember, a polygraph machine doesn't actually measure truth, which means that if a suspect can manipulate the test's measurement of physiological functions associated with lying, the results can be significantly influenced to produce a false result. And keep in mind that a sociopath with no conscience doesn't feel much of anything when he lies, so he can falsely pass a test without even rigging it. In the infamous murder investigation known as the Utah Church Bombings case, for example, the suspect initially said he was innocent, and polygraph results supported his claim. But the guy ultimately pleaded guilty. I don't know if the guy was a sociopath, but I'm certain his polygraph test produced a false result.

John and Patsy Ramsey claimed that a polygraph proved their innocence, too, though they didn't even take one until some three years after JonBenet was murdered. Any honest defense attorney will tell you that guilty criminals never take polygraphs right away because, although most people can eventually learn how to beat the machine, it's a whole lot easier to pull off a false result two or three years after the crime when emotions fade, and you've had time to find the right "expert" and learn how to beat the machine.

When the Ramseys finally did hire someone to give them a polygraph test, the first result was reportedly inconclusive. After another test, they claimed to have passed, but the full details have never been revealed; and the little that is known suggests the test was conducted under conditions that were not designed to produce a reliable result.

For example, a proper question should be short, to the point, and it shouldn't contain words that have loose meanings, or ask about a person's state of mind. For example, a good question would be, "Did you kill JonBenet?" Not much wriggle room there. The Ramseys were asked long and murky questions like, "Did you inflict any of the injuries that caused the death of JonBenet?" And, "Regarding JonBenet, did you inflict any of the injuries that caused her death?" And, "Regarding JonBenet, do you know for sure who killed her?"

Adding extra words and fuzzy terms like "regarding," "for sure," "inflict," and "injuries" is not appropriate because it gives the mind of the test subject time and definitional "space" to wander. Short, direct questions are better because the subject is forced to focus on a single topic, precisely stated.

The test is also dependent on the nature of the "known truthful" standard, which refers to the machine's measurement of a person's response to a question everyone knows was answered truthfully. This measurement becomes the standard by which questions about guilt are measured. If the "known truthful" question is more of a murky half-truth than a simple and direct declaration, then lies about guilt will look more like a truthful answer. For example, if the known truthful standard is, "Did you recently move to Main Street," and the truth is, you moved to Main Street six months ago, the "known truthful" standard would be diminished by the murkiness of the word "recently." If this is then compared to a similarly murky question about guilt such as "Regarding JonBenet, do you know for certain who killed her?"; the answer "no" might well produce a measurement that resembles the "known truthful" standard even if the answer "no" is a lie.

We also don't know whether the Ramseys learned some of the more well-known tricks people use to beat the machine. For example, suspects sometimes put a tack in their shoe, and poke it with their toe when a "known truthful" question is asked, such as, "Is your name John?" The pain causes an increase in heart rate and perspiration, which shows up as a measurement of "truth" on the machine's printout. If the suspect then experiences an increase in heart rate and perspiration *without* stepping on the tack, when he falsely says, "No" in response to a question about whether he committed a crime, the answer will appear truthful because it will match the measurement of the "known truthful" question.

Full details of the Ramseys' test conditions have not been released, although the examiner in that case admitted that he did not require the Ramseys to submit to a drug test to determine whether they were under the influence of any substance that might have affected their physiological responses at the time of the test.

We also don't know what the pretest interview of the Ramseys was like or whether there *was* one. John Nasuti says this is an important part of the process because it allows the examiner to get the suspect focused on the matter at hand. During the pretest interview, the examiner reveals his awareness of the facts of case - including the most damning evidence - so that the suspect is aware that the examiner will notice even the slightest deception. This also gets the test subject thinking about the details of the crime, which helps produce a more reliable result.

Maybe most interesting about the Ramseys' polygraph test is that they refused to submit to an FBI-administered test, even after promising on national television that they would do anything asked of them. I have no way of knowing whether the Ramseys' test results are legitimate, but too many important questions remain unanswered, and it's suspicious for anyone who refuses to submit to a police-administered examination to claim publicly that they've been proved innocent by a polygraph test.

Paid experts are everywhere in our legal system, and they usually provide a valuable service to the court because they offer specialized knowledge to help jurors better understand unusual, complicated or highly technical evidence. But in too many cases, when the defense hires an expert, the goal is not elucidation but distortion of the truth. It's hard for jurors and the general public to be skeptical of experts because we generally assume that a professional with a degree would never lie for money. But many hired guns persuade themselves that they aren't fudging tests, or lying so much as providing a speculative alternative explanation for damning evidence. They can call it what they want. It's often lies for money.

Our justice system needs a way to keep the gates open wide enough so that experts are allowed in, but not so wide that frauds and tricksters walk through, too. Without strict standards, we will continue to see lies and distortion, and taxpayers' dollars will go to waste as indigent defendants insist on being handed the public's money to hire experts willing to lie for cash. Even the not-so-indigent find ways to waste the public's money on hired guns. Scott Peterson's defense team scored over $225,000 in tax dollars to hire a group of experts, not one of whom actually helped. Professional licensing boards have to set better ethical standards to stop experts from misstating or manipulating the truth in judicial proceedings.

The public has had its fill of hired guns in the courtroom, as illustrated by the growing number of lawsuits against experts. Some lawyers decry the trend as unfortunate, but lawsuits help inspire all experts in all fields, including polygraph examiners, to think twice before taking a big fee to fudge the truth.

We can all help prevent these scams by being skeptical when we hear defense attorneys make self-serving announcements about their clients passing polygraphs. We need to listen hard to the details and ask important questions like: What were the test conditions? How much was the expert paid? Were the questions short and direct, or long and murky? Did the suspect ingest any drugs or intoxicating substances before the test? How long after the crime was the polygraph test done? Did the suspect refuse law enforcement's request to conduct its own polygraph? Did the suspect learn how to rig the test? Is the expert willing to release the details of all the test conditions? Were police allowed to be present for the test? Were they allowed to inspect the machine and otherwise assess the test conditions?

Unless we get answers to all these questions, when a suspect says he passed a polygraph with flying colors, we should assume that it wasn't much of a test at all, and that he didn't pass it so much as participate in a charade. And trust me, there were no flying colors involved.

FIFTEEN

Mounting the "Not the Criminal Type" Defense

What do the following two defense attorneys have in common? First, there's the lawyer who argued that his sexy blonde client, who raped her male high school student, was "too pretty" to go to prison. And, then, there's Scott Peterson's first lawyer, who let Peterson do television interviews before trial in the hope his "boy next door" look might sway public opinion and influence potential jurors not to convict.

The answer: Both lawyers mounted a "not the criminal type" defense.

It's not a new trick. It's one that's been in our faces for a long time, but it seems to be gaining in popularity and undermining justice now more than ever before. No doubt the Internet and 24/7 news coverage has increased its popularity, which means it's time we took a closer look so we can better resist this nonsense.

Supporters of Michael Jackson used this trick during his child sex abuse trial by arguing he wasn't the "type" who molests children. "He loves children too much," they claimed. After all, he built a zoo and an amusement park in his front yard, and spent all his time with kids. Doesn't that put him above suspicion?

Um, not quite.

Most of us saw Jackson's obsession with kids as a strong indicator that he was *exactly* the "type" to molest children, though a few observers made the reasonable point that Jackson wasn't a "classic molester" because real pedophiles are sneaky, and usually try hard *not* to "look" the part. In other words, they're not dumb enough to keep child-bait in the front yard!

While the public was debating whether men who build zoos in their front yard are molester "types," Jackson's lawyers were fighting hard to prevent the jury from hearing the most powerful evidence of what "type" the pop star really was. The prosecution wanted to use evidence that Jackson abused many children, but the defense said such evidence would be unfair because it would make jurors think Jackson was a molester "type." Well, yeah.

The defense insisted, however, that jurors be allowed to hear about the carnival rides on Jackson's front lawn, so they would see that he wasn't the molester "type." See how it works? It's O.K. to use stereotypes, so long as they work to the advantage of the criminal. Even hard evidence that shows an offender's pattern of dangerous behavior, which isn't a stereotype at all, is somehow unfair, but the accused has a Constitutional right to use merry-go-rounds to falsely suggest innocence.

There's no such thing as a "criminal type," and most crime victims are hurt by people who don't look scary at all. Ted Bundy, after all, could have been a male model, and Neil Entwistle, the British guy convicted in 2008 of executing his wife and baby daughter in Hopkinton, Massachusetts, looked like Dream Date Ken. And let's not forget Alex and Derek King, the two Justin Beiber look-a-likes from Florida who slaughtered their father in cold blood.

It's a real problem that judges too often let criminals exploit the fact that they don't "look like" criminals while prohibiting prosecutors from rebutting this theatrical tactic by using evidence that shows exactly the type of monster the defendant really is.

In New York State, an attorney and married father of two was prosecuted for raping his son's friend. John Seaman claimed at his trial that he wasn't "the type" who would be interested in, much less rape, a teenage boy. To rebut this, the prosecutor let the jury know that Seaman was, indeed the "type" because he had groomed the boy by giving him alcohol, showing him pornography, and engaging in other behaviors inconsistent with the ordinary behavior of a married attorney and father of two children. The jury convicted the guy.

So far, so good. But then an appellate court overturned the conviction because it was "too prejudicial" to let the jury hear about the booze and the porn because the jury might have thought the guy was a sleaze ball. But it was the truth, and it was the prosecution's job to let the jury know how a perpetrator groomed a child before the abuse happened. Why should jurors be misled to believe that a guy is a normal, upright, law-abiding citizen if the truth is otherwise? A jury should not hear unfair evidence, but neither should they be allowed to acquit a man based on the erroneous assumption that he isn't the criminal "type."

Scott Peterson went down this road, too. He gave an interview to Diane Sawyer and managed to get a stream of tears flowing down his boy-next-door cheeks, while his creaky voice spewed one lie after the next. Not the type, indeed! Many people didn't understand that they were being played by a guy who wasn't man enough to answer police questions, but didn't mind yakking up a storm with a journalist who, by force of circumstance, wasn't in a position to ask the brutal questions cops would have asked if they could have - questions that would have cooked his goose, quick.

Defense attorneys think it's acceptable for a criminal to talk to the press, but not to the cops, because the Fifth

Amendment says nothing about talking to or even *lying* to the media, the public, or by extension, all potential jurors. Defense attorneys don't care that the sacred Fifth Amendment has become a mockery, allowing criminals to remain *selectively* silent while exploiting all other means to undermine justice, taint the jury pool and corruptly influence the investigation. This craziness costs taxpayers a fortune because when a criminal fills the airwaves with silly statements about other suspects and theories about who else could have committed the crime, law enforcement officials have to run off on wild goose chases trying to disprove the false claims so that jurors down the road won't wonder whether cops ruled out that "suspicious sighting" or angry ex-boyfriend.

This practice of criminals messing up investigations and "testifying without taking the stand" wouldn't work if the public had no interest in the case. But we can't seem to help being riveted by cases where the perpetrator doesn't seem to be the criminal "type." See the conundrum? The Petersons of the world can whip up a mob of misguided supporters by playing against our expectations, and we help them do it by paying attention!

I understand why people are fascinated by certain cases. It's scary to imagine Scott Peterson as the "type" of person who could slaughter his wife and nearly born son. If he's the "killer type," how can we protect ourselves and our children from dangerous people? How can we figure out who the "safe" people are, if seemingly "safe" people look like Scott Peterson? This is terrifying stuff to most people, and defense attorneys know it, which is why they exploit our fears whenever they can in the hope of generating reasonable doubt.

Most people can respect the right to remain silent, but when a suspect refuses to speak to police, then makes false claims of innocence to the press, respect for the Bill of Rights takes a hit. Criminals who take the Fifth should be required to *shut up*. No television, no radio, no BS about wanting to find "the real killer." Zip it!

More than ever before, with 24/7 news coverage of high-profile trials, the public airwaves are saturated with bogus information and defense attorney pundits who spin the lies. The inevitable results? Important cases are decided more like beauty contests than serious legal controversies. No case was more disturbing on this point than the celebratory coverage of child rapist Mary Kay Letourneau.

Letourneau was a grade school teacher and married mother of four young children when she decided to become "sexually involved" with her twelve-year-old student, Villi Fulaau. She raped Fulaau when he was thirteen, got caught, then got herself in trouble again when she became pregnant by Fulaau when he wasn't remotely old enough to make a mature decision about lunch, much less sex with an adult or the serious nature of fatherhood. Letourneau didn't care. She repeatedly defied the court's orders to stay away from Fulaau, which landed her back in prison where she gave birth to another of Fulaau's children. When she finally got out for good, Fulaau was old enough to make his own decisions, and he married Letourneau. Some people talk about the situation like it's a Romeo and Juliet love story for the ages. But most of us wonder why Letourneau was allowed to keep custody of the two babies born of her crimes?

What kind of court system rewards child sex offenders with the gift of parenthood? What will she tell her children when they ask about how they were born? "Well, dear, you see, when your daddy was a boy, I was his teacher and I raped him – and that's how I became pregnant with you." So sweet. Who's going to pay the bill for the children's lifetime of mental health care? And think about this: There's nothing the children can do to move to a safe neighborhood – away from convicted sex offenders!

All this stuff happened, in part, because we think biology and birth trump everything and that, if a rapist is a woman and the victim is a teenage boy, it can't be that bad. In fact, studies show that male victims of teacher abuse suffer terribly as adults, no matter how good the body parts feel at the time of the crime, because of the betrayal involved when an adult in a position of authority exploits a child's trust. Schoolboys have many hormonal things going on in their bodies, and they lack the maturity to protect themselves from adults willing to take advantage. Kids have always had crushes on their teachers, but good teachers know it's not real love, and they leave the kids alone out of respect for the their immaturity. Letourneau was not a good teacher.

Letourneau had the advantage of looking like little Lindy Loo from the Whos down in Whoville? How could a sweet-looking mother of four be *that* "dangerous," right? Again, the joke's on us because we think we know by looking at her what "type" of person she really is, and with the benefit of relentless televised romanticization of the whole mess, we cut her slack she didn't deserve. Shame on us. We should have been smart enough to look beyond the doe-eyed glances and pixie hairdo, to see her as nothing more than a woman who sexually exploited a child to satisfy her criminal fantasies.

News coverage of trials involving suspects who are "not the criminal type" can be a good thing. After all, Scott Peterson hurt his own case by making statements to the press that were then used to prove his guilt. And when we're paying attention to a case like that, even for the wrong reasons, it helps us see more clearly that a nice-looking guy could be a not-so-nice human being.

But we need to work harder to stop criminals from misusing the press to thwart justice. When a guy like Scott Peterson won't talk to detectives, he should be forbidden to talk to Diane Sawyer. At the very least, someone in

Sawyer's position should make it clear during the broadcast of the interview that the guy has asserted his right to remain silent with cops. The public has a right to know when they're being used.

Meanwhile, we can't let our gut-level fears about seemingly nice people being criminal "types" trump our capacity to use common sense and logic when we see a good-looking person accused of a brutal crime. We need to give up a little bit of our desire to feel safe all the time and get more comfortable with the discomfort of knowing that pretty people, rich people, and celebrated people are capable of very bad things. Accepting that a guy who looks like Scott Peterson could be a dangerous monster doesn't mean he *is* dangerous, and it doesn't mean that every handsome guy will one day kill his wife, but would it be so terrible if we made people *earn* our trust with their actions rather than *giving away* our trust because of their appearance?

It's O.K. to be a bit more suspicious of the guy next door – even if he does look like Dream Date Ken.

SIXTEEN

Blaming the Victim

All life is precious. We can probably agree on that.

Every person, no matter how poor, unlucky, or downtrodden, deserves a shot at happiness. By extension, nobody deserves to be a crime victim. Yes, we all have to take steps to protect ourselves and avoid engaging in risky behavior. But that doesn't mean if we make a bad choice, we're somehow responsible for the criminal behavior of someone else.

We don't always remember this when bad things happen to people with troubled lives, or to those who weren't doing their best to protect themselves when something terrible happened. All too often, we blame the victim by reacting with indignation and harsh judgments when we hear, for example, that a woman was having fun and drinking alcohol before she was raped. Or when a child is kidnapped, we ask where the parents were, instead of criticizing the perpetrator, as if something the parents did *entitled* the kidnapper to take the child.

This is terribly unfair, and it makes no sense if we want to get tough on the bad guys. Let me be blunt. There's only 100 percent of blame to go around when crime happens. For every bit of blame we place on the victim, we necessarily reduce the criminal's responsibility. Do we really want to give a robber a break because he picked on a guy who got drunk at a bar with coworkers before the crime?

Remember Imette St. Guillen, the woman I wrote about in chapter thirteen who was murdered in New York by a bouncer at a bar near her home? A loud bunch of hateful people in this country said she was partly to blame for her own death because she went to a bar alone, late at night. But she didn't hurt anybody or do anything illegal. Our outrage should be saved for the evil monsters who torture, rape, and murder innocent victims.

Who in their right mind would want a judge or a jury to cut a criminal slack for kidnapping a child? But that's exactly what happens in the courtroom when victims are blamed for someone else's criminal behavior. Taken to its logical next step, people hit by drunk drivers are partly to blame because they could have stayed home. See how dumb it is.

There's no way to prevent a dangerous person from committing a crime. And if an innocent person just happens to be in the bad guy's path when the criminal mood strikes, it's not the victim's fault. I don't care if a woman strips naked and does cartwheels down the middle of Main Street, rape is always wrong. And I don't care if the elderly owner of a corner store never got around to installing a security camera. It's *only* the robber's fault if he takes advantage of the situation and robs the storeowner blind.

I'll go even further: When people have problems, I see them as the underdogs, and I want the criminals who pick on them to be punished *extra* harshly, not given a discount for picking on the weak. Maybe you don't agree with this but the next time you're tempted to blame a victim, ask yourself whether the criminal jumped at the chance to pick on someone who couldn't defend herself and then ask yourself if it makes sense to go easy on that kind of perpetrator. Then, remember what I told you about why sex predators pick on kids.

I've worked on cases involving victims from all walks of life, and I can't think of a single person who deserved to be hurt. Even when pedophile priest John Geoghan was murdered in a Massachusetts prison by a man who said he did it to avenge all the harm Geoghan caused to so many children, I spoke out against that crime. I said exactly what I'm saying here: Nobody *deserves* to be a crime victim.

Our unfortunate propensity to judge victims harshly is the flip side of our similarly unfortunate inclination to feel sympathy when a celebrity or influential politician stands accused of a crime. We blame the victims when they have difficult lives, and we forgive the guilty when their lives are charmed. Go figure.

One thing I've noticed in more than twenty years working with victims is that when I look into their eyes and see the pain, it looks exactly the same whether the victim is rich or poor, and no matter how troubled their lives had been before the crime, which is why all crime victims deserve our sympathy *and* our support. Yet we don't treat all victims with equal respect. We elevate some and look down on others as if some people deserve to be abused.

At the same time, the bad guy gets compassion, legal assistance, help from expert witnesses and the support of mental health professionals who want us to feel bad for the guy, or at least understand how he went from cuddly little baby to rapist or murderer.

I do think we should care about why people are violent, mainly so we can look for ways to head off similar downward spirals in the future. But I'm not interested in the perpetrator's problems to the exclusion of even one ounce of compassion for the victim. That's where I get off the bus. The simple fact is the bad guy has been charged with a crime, and the victim has been injured. One person committed a terrible act of violence, and the other is in pain as a result. Compassion, support and understanding should go first and foremost to the one in pain.

In our weird culture, the legal system is literally *designed* to add to a victim's suffering by allowing perpetrators and their lawyers to build up defense strategies by tearing down the victim.

I'm not kidding. In some states, defense attorneys file motions to stop victims from even uttering the word "victim" in court because a jury might presume the guy's guilt when they hear the word. Of course, the real reason is, if defense attorneys can stop victims from referring to themselves as victims, jurors could well vote to acquit simply because they think it's weird that a victim wouldn't describe herself as a "victim" during the trial.

Judges go along with such dopey arguments even though it's a violation of the First Amendment for a judge to censor the words a victim uses to describe the crime. She has the right to call herself a ham sandwich if she wants to, but most victims don't understand that they even *have* First Amendment rights during trial, and most advocates don't tell victims about their rights, much less how to enforce them.

Think I'm exaggerating? Kobe Bryant's lawyers filed a motion demanding that the victim be ordered not to use the word "victim" during trial and the judge allowed it. Though it was clearly an illegal order, nobody did a damn thing about it - not the prosecutor, not the judge, not the victim's private attorney. Nobody objected or pointed out to the judge that he had no authority to censor the victim's descriptive language in court. But it gets worse: A group of people at a nearby rape crisis center *agreed with the defense* that the victim should be forbidden to use the word "victim." Half the staff at the Colorado Coalition Against Sexual Assault even quit their jobs in protest over the fact that their own organization had used the word "victim" in statements they issued to the media in support of the woman Bryant attacked.

Crazy, right?! Rape "victim" advocates insisting that a rape "victim" not be allowed to call herself a "victim" because it imposes on Bryant's presumption of innocence! Someone should have told those nuts to take a second look at the sign on their door. They did not work at the Colorado Coalition for *Defendants' Rights*. Their job is to advocate for "victims," which means they're allowed to call the people they help *victims*.

Someone should have made the simple point that when a victim or a rape crisis center uses the word "victim," it does not violate the presumption of innocence. Unless you're the judge or a juror, you can use whatever words you want, and you can presume guilt all day long.

What crime victim *doesn't* presume the guilt of their attacker the moment the crime happens and every day thereafter? Most of us presume O.J. Simpson's guilt even though he was acquitted, as well we should. And who among us would send our kids to a neighbor's house for milk and cookies if the guy was accused, but not yet convicted, of child rape? Unfair? Not at all. Being charged with a crime may not provide proof of culpability beyond a reasonable doubt, but it does provide a reason for suspicion.

A lot of vetting goes on before criminal charges are filed because prosecutors don't like taking on cases they can't win. In fact, it's unethical to file a case without a good faith belief that the charges can be proved beyond a reasonable doubt.

This doesn't mean the presumption of innocence is unimportant. It's simply a reminder that the rule applies in the courtroom, not the real world.

But we have to be careful, too, because if we're going to judge people harshly in the real world, we have to be extra conscientious about the presumption of innocence when we sit in judgment of others as jurors. I'd probably be an especially good juror in a criminal case because I'd be worried about my own biases, and I'd go overboard to compensate. We all have to be fair in the courtroom, no matter what judgments we make about people in the real world. If only the defense bar and their ideological allies could understand the importance of being fair to victims the way I worry about being fair to criminals.

The criminal justice system is not the sole arbiter of truth. The suffering of victims is real even if a jury votes "not guilty." Judges, as agents of the government, should respect the feelings of people who have suffered criminal harm, and allow them to use their own words to describe what happened. Let the jury decide what to make of someone's word choice.

And let's be serious for a minute. The word "victim" is no more unfair to an accused criminal than the word "witness," because if the word "victim" presumes that a person suffered harm, then the word "witness" presumes that a person saw what they say they saw. Even the word "arrest" is a problem because it presumes that police had probable cause to believe that a crime occurred. I could go on. When the power of a word is problematic, the judge should simply instruct the jury not to give it unfair weight.

Fairness for the accused is important, but let's get off the high horse. Defense attorneys want to outlaw the word "victim," not because it's unfair but because they prefer the words "accuser" and "complainant." These mean-sounding words wrongly suggest that the *victim* instead of the *government*, filed the charges, which takes away any sense that law enforcement officials validated the claims and determined the evidence was strong enough for criminal prosecution. The victim is not the "accuser" or a "complainant," she is a witness for the state, and when criminal charges are filed it means the government investigated the case and validated the victim's credibility. Defense attorneys know that if jurors think about a criminal trial as the government's case, they are more likely to believe the victim, which is why they try so hard to separate the victim from the prosecution. It's not a problem with the word "victim" so much as a tactical effort to trick the jury into thinking the prosecutor isn't necessarily on the victim's side.

The power of human drama in the courtroom can trump basic common sense and sound logic easily because, as I said, too many jurors are idiots. So defense attorneys do whatever they can to take advantage. I've even seen rape cases where the defense used rape-shield laws to *hurt* victims. Think about that. Shield laws are supposed to *protect* victims from having their credibility attacked during trial with evidence of past sexual activities. But many defense attorneys use these *protective* laws to help guilty rapists go free.

I may be the only lawyer in the country with the guts to say this out loud, but I think we should rip rape-shield laws out of the book altogether because they hurt victims more than they help. Think I'm kidding? Get this: In the Kobe Bryant case, the victim was forced to testify at a pretrial hearing about all sorts of irrelevant things related to her past sexual conduct. And who forced her to do this, you wonder? The defense, of course. And why was this allowed to happen? Because the rape-shield law in Colorado says that a defense attorney must file a motion in *advance* of trial if he wants to offer evidence of a victim's past sex life *during* the trial. The judge is then required to conduct a hearing to determine whether the evidence will be admitted. Bryant's defense team argued that because the law requires a hearing *about* the victim's sex life, they had a right to subpoena the victim to the hearing and ask whatever they wanted *about* her sex life. Putting aside the absurdity of a judge allowing the law to be turned on its head this way, the bottom line is that, in about a dozen states, shield laws are being misused by defense attorneys to conduct exactly these sorts of outrageous and illegal fishing expeditions.

Let me make this clear: If there had been no rape-shield law in Colorado, Bryant's lawyers never could have forced the victim to appear at a hearing and answer questions about her sex life. If Bryant had been accused of robbing or beating the victim, rather than raping her, there wouldn't have been a hearing at all because there's no such thing as a robbery-shield law to protect victims from having to answer questions about their prior philanthropy habits. Just rape victims. Just rape-shield laws.

It's time to get rid of these laws altogether and ask judges to start doing their jobs. Rape shield laws were created a long time ago because too many judges were being unfair to victims, ruling all sexual history evidence as relevant in every case. They would make silly rulings like "if she consented in the past, she probably consented on the night in question." Shield laws were enacted to kick these judges in the head a little bit, to get them to understand that no matter how many times a victim had sex in the past, it tells us nothing about whether she consented on the night in question. More than thirty years later, shield laws have morphed into rules that are more harmful than helpful, and it's time to get rid of them before another victim is *violated* by a law that was supposed to *protect* her from unfair treatment in court.

Misusing a victim's sexual past as a trial strategy doesn't only affect rape victims. It comes up in all types of cases where the defense can gain points by shaming the victim about sex. It happened to Brenda and Damon Van Dam, the parents of seven-year-old Danielle, who was kidnapped from her home and brutally murdered by a disgusting guy named David Westerfield.

Westerfield's attorney, Steven Feldman, the guy I told you about in chapter nine, knew that he had a vicious animal for a client. The evidence against Westerfield was overwhelming. But rather than challenging the evidence and making sure his client got a fair trial, he did exactly the thing that makes people hate defense attorneys. He tried to blame Danielle's mother and father for the crime by telling the jury that their lifestyle - they were accused of being swingers and pot smokers - could have enabled one of their undesirable buddies to steal Danielle from her bed.

If the prosecutor had dared imply that Westerfield was a pig, which he was, the defense would have thrown a hissy fit and insisted that the case be dismissed to punish the prosecutor for making derogatory remarks. But the defense could say whatever it wanted about a family that was already heartbroken beyond comprehension, even though nothing they did in their private lives had anything to do with the crime. There was not a scintilla of evidence that anyone but Westerfield committed the crime, yet the defense was allowed to pretend that some unknown boogeyman killed the child, and that the parents were responsible because they had an unusual lifestyle.

In the more recent case of Jodi Arias, a seemingly sweet young woman accused of savagely killing her ex-boyfriend, Travis Alexander, the defense team spent a lot of time talking about Travis' fondness for oral sex. The defense claimed it was one of the reasons Arias had to kill the guy in self-defense. Mind you, she planned the killing, drove from California to Arizona with the murder weapons, stabbed him nearly *thirty* times in the back, and almost sliced his head off with a deep and long cut to the throat. Then she shot him in the head.

Arias initially told cops she had nothing to do with the murder and had no idea what happened. Then she said two strangers killed Travis, and she boasted on a news program that no jury would ever convict her.

At trial, she admitted killing Travis alone and claimed it was self-defense.

It's fine to assert even a ridiculous defense, but the defense spent days talking about Travis' sex life. Some of the stuff wasn't even true, and none of it explained thirty stab wounds, a near decapitation and multiple lies to cops about what really happened.

Our justice system allows defense attorneys not only to make stuff up, but also, to rub salt in the wounds of people in pain. Maybe you think mounting a vigorous defense means pulling out all the stops, and that there should be no limits to what the defense can say and do in the name of justice. But I don't think you can make the case that judges have no choice but to allow cruel strategies that needlessly put victims and their families through legal meat grinders, and that these vile strategies are necessary to protect the rights of the accused.

The Van Dams could have been as perfect as the Von Trapps in *The Sound of Music*, and it would not have mattered. Westerfield would have kidnapped and murdered little Danielle because he was an evil man, period. That the parents had unusual private lives is just as irrelevant as the fact that the Von Trapps were delightfully perfect. But the defense didn't care. The judge didn't care. The parents were violated repeatedly for no reason except that the defense team saw a strategic upside in slamming them to the pavement.

Some jurors allow defense attorneys to manipulate them into believing that parents bear some of the responsibility when a child is kidnapped or killed. It makes them feel better about themselves. If they harshly judge a child's parents, they can psychologically distance themselves from the pain of the parents whose child was taken. It makes them think *their* children will never be kidnapped.

But it's not only delusional to believe bad parents somehow "cause" criminals to kidnap children, it's wrong as a matter of law. The idea of shared blame is inapplicable in the criminal justice system. Unlike a civil suit for money, in which one person might be 30 percent responsible, another 40 percent, and so on, in a criminal case, there's no such thing as comparative negligence or shared responsibility.

In a criminal courtroom, it's an all or nothing deal. Either the bad guy is 100 percent guilty, or he isn't. There's no "partly guilty" option on the verdict form.

Why am I thumping away on this point? Because this simple mathematical truth explains why the defense has no *right* to put forth evidence at trial that blames or shames the victim or the victim's parents, or anyone else.

The only time defense attorneys don't try to blame victims and their families is when those attorneys think the victims can provide something useful to the defense. When Matthew Shepard was brutally beaten to death in 1998 by a group of young men who targeted him because he was gay, the defense didn't attack his family, or suggest the boy might still be alive if his mother had been a better parent by not letting him go out the night he was killed. This is because Shepard's mother, amazingly enough, announced soon after her son's murder that she did not want the prosecutor to seek the death penalty even though the prosecutor wanted death to be an option for the cowardly killers. The defense not only didn't try to blame Shepard's mother for her son's death, they put her on a pedestal and sang her praises. It was a virtual love fest, with the defense going on and on about how the victim's mother should be honored and respected for her feelings about the death penalty.

Of course, if Shepard's mother had said the opposite, that justice in her son's case called for the ultimate punishment, the defense almost certainly would have argued that she was a vindictive witch who was acting out of her own feelings of guilt. They would have blamed her for not protecting her son from the animals who killed him, and they would have screamed and yelled that victims have no business dictating the killer's punishment because murder is the government's business, not the victim's private lawsuit, and so on.

Blaming victims not only adds insult to the injuries of people who have already suffered terribly, it also creates a hierarchy of human value because it suggests that certain types of people deserve a better form of justice. This is dangerous thinking. All things about life are not equal, but nobody deserves to be raped or murdered because of who they are in society, or because of how they lived their lives.

Think of it this way: If blaming *some* types of victims is acceptable, Rush Limbaugh will have a tough time with the legal system if he's ever victimized by crime. Why? Because the defense will argue his past drug addiction undermines his credibility. Tipper Gore will have trouble, too, because she's suffered from depression. Patrick Kennedy won't be treated fairly because he's been to rehab. And forget about Lindsay Lohan and Britney Spears. All these people are more at risk for crime because they are hopelessly vulnerable to blame-the-victim strategies.

Everyone has problems, and I'm not saying we shouldn't be careful and take steps to protect ourselves and our children from violence. But if we don't want to reward criminals who pick on the weak, we have to talk openly and often about how human flaws are *vulnerabilities*, not *liabilities*.

Consider the case of kidnap victim Shawn Hornbeck, the eleven-year-old Missouri boy who was found in 2007 after being held for four years by a man named Michael Devlin. The public was quick to raise an eyebrow about why the child didn't escape during his captivity. He had many opportunities to flee because Devlin sometimes left the boy home alone, and Hornbeck spent time at friends' houses. He even had a cellphone and once reported a stolen bike to the police, but didn't tell them he'd been kidnapped. This makes no sense to most people who wonder whether Hornbeck liked living with Devlin.

Maybe the boy was glad to be kidnapped because it got him away from other problems at home. On the other hand, it's possible the boy was suffering from what experts call "child abuse accommodation syndrome," a term that describes what terrified kids do when they feel helpless and learn to adapt to abuse and accept their circumstances as normal because they don't have the maturity to understand what's happening, or the power to get out of harm's way. Once abuse becomes incorporated into their brains as normal, they don't even think about running away. They accept that being abused is part of life. Is it any wonder that sometimes these kids grow up and abuse others?

As rational adults, jurors don't understand why a victim wouldn't leave at the first opportunity, or, at the very least, tell someone. Most people don't have the life experience to fairly assess what looks to them like very strange behavior. They judge the victim by their *own* lives, and if they can't wrap their heads around how the victim behaved, they reject it as irrational.

It doesn't really matter whether Shawn Hornbeck was glad to be away from his family because even if the boy had run away from a troubled home life and begged Devlin to let him stay, Devlin had no right to keep the child. Period. Most people understand this idea in the abstract, but they don't apply the idea in the real world.

If we don't start being fair to victims, defense attorneys will continue to dredge up and sling the mud whenever smearing the victim might win points for the criminal at trial. I don't know about you but I don't like landing by default on the side of the perpetrator because some defense attorney pulled me away from the victim with propaganda about why he or she isn't very likable, or didn't do a good enough job protecting herself from harm.

From now on, when we hear a defense attorney say something insulting about a victim, let's at least agree to recognize the ploy as unfair manipulation. Remember

(Wendy) Murphy's Law: The blame game won't work if we don't let it.

SEVENTEEN

Legislating Nothingness and Confusion

When Bill O'Reilly hired me to work with him on his Jessica's Law campaign, the first thing I did was try to get a handle on what the laws looked like in all fifty states. After a couple of hours of research, my head was spinning - and this is my field of expertise!

Simply understanding the definitions of "child sex crimes" was a struggle. Across our 50 states, there are more than 30 distinct terms to describe the single act of child rape. From "lewd act" to "molestation" to "sexual abuse," we can't even agree on what to call it.

Making laws complicated and incomprehensible is a terrible dirty trick that benefits the perpetrators. Why? Because if we can't readily determine what was done to a child by the very title of the crime, it's harder to get outraged when we hear that a perpetrator got a meager sentence. In other words, it's harder to fight for justice if we have no idea whether justice was served.

Demystifying all this stuff, and getting the public on board to help the laws work better for kids, is why Bill O'Reilly started his Jessica's Law campaign in the first place. After a few years of O'Reilly making the protection of children a priority on his Fox News show, *The O'Reilly Factor*, politicians stepped up and started passing new laws. Bill singlehandedly made it happen, but it wasn't easy. Lawmakers, judges, prosecutors and defense attorneys went into hiding when Bill asked them to defend a decision that put a predator back on the street. The few who tried to explain themselves often blamed the law itself as the reason the perpetrator was set free. This wasn't usually true, but if the laws were more uniform and easier to understand, the public would be in a better position to hold officials responsible.

Laws are often intentionally designed to obfuscate and confuse the public, precisely so that people who care about protecting children will have a tougher time figuring out what went wrong, and what needs fixing.

In North Carolina, for example, the law states that rape of a child under age thirteen carries a mandatory punishment of twelve years in prison. But in another section of the law, a section that isn't mentioned in the part that talks about "mandatory" punishment, judges are given the authority to reduce the "mandatory" punishment if they find "extraordinary mitigation." This section is *not* supposed to apply to the crime of child rape, but if a prosecutor allows the perpetrator to plead to a lesser-included offense (which happens *all* the time), the mandatory sentence law has no applicability. The rapist can be set free on probation, even though the law says he should be in prison for a minimum of twelve years and even though the good people of North Carolina voted for politicians who *said* they enacted *truly mandatory sentencing* laws in their criminal code.

In Washington State, the law that describes the punishment for rape of a child says the crime carries a *mandatory* term of five years in prison, but another statute, in an entirely other section, says it's only a "presumptive" guideline, not a mandate. Serial rapist and child murderer

Joseph Duncan was convicted of his first sex offense against a child in the state of Washington, but because he received a woefully inadequate punishment, he was allowed to roam free, which enabled him to kidnap Dylan and Shasta Grohne. Duncan eventually murdered Shasta and though Dylan survived, he suffered terribly. If Washington's laws worked the way they were intended, and the way the public thought they were *supposed* to work, the Grohne kids would have been spared unimaginable horror.

In Indiana, the law says that rape of a child carries a *mandatory* term of twenty years. But "twenty" actually means "ten," because another law gives automatic credit to the criminal such that the sentence is immediately reduced by half, and with earned "good time" credits for good behavior, the perpetrator can get out even sooner. The saddest part is that that while the innocent public thinks they have "tough" laws, the Indiana child rapists know the real deal. They know "twenty" means "ten" or less. And they factor this into the cost of doing harm to kids.

It's bad enough that child predators already avoid getting caught in most cases simply by threatening to kill the child's mother or pet rabbit, etc. When they calculate the low risk of ever getting caught, together with the promise of no more than a wrist-slap from the legal system, they offend repeatedly. On behalf of the kids in Indiana, thanks a lot.

When I first started researching the laws for Bill O'Reilly, fewer than half the states had any *real* mandatory punishments for child rapists. After only one year of Bill's Jessica's Law campaign, forty states had either enacted a mandatory sentence law, or had made a firm commitment to getting such a law passed. This was a phenomenal result and an effort that other news programs should imitate as an essential public service. Kids don't vote, and on the whole, they don't have any money. They need the media's help to make sure government officials expend appropriate resources to protect them from harm.

O'Reilly understands this. He knows the media has a responsibility to give an extra voice to those who cannot speak for themselves. As an advocate for kids for more than twenty years, I understand it, too. I see the duplicitous faces of politicians who talk a good talk on television about "protecting the kids," only to vote in secret *against* the enactment of laws that would actually protect children from harm. This is a particularly insidious problem when elected officials double dip as defense lawyers because they routinely indulge the desires of their criminal clients over the needs of their vulnerable constituents.

We need to start holding devious elected officials accountable for the sneaky things they do *after* the news cameras are gone. And we need to pay closer attention when a seemingly good law is stuffed with the kind of loopholes that render the law useless on the day of it's enactment. At a minimum, we need smarter leadership in the victim advocacy community to make sure lawmakers aren't selling us a pig in a poke. For example, nonprofits that purport to be doing policy work for victims should have statutory construction analysts on staff to make sure that a proposed law that looks good on the outside isn't a wolf in sheep's clothing. Something as benign as the use of the word "may" instead of "shall" can turn a legal mandate into a mere suggestion.

If we're ever going to hold lawmakers and other public officials accountable, our sex-crimes laws need to be simplified. At a minimum, information about all convicted sex offenders should be publicly available on the Internet, *including exactly what they did, as well as the titles of the crimes for which they were convicted.* When the public reads a news story, they need to know more than whether the perpetrator was convicted of "molestation" because this could mean a one-time pat on a child's rear end, or multiple acts of sodomy. And sex offender registries should be revamped so that a certain "level" of "dangerousness" means the same thing in all fifty states.

This is important in a crazy state like Massachusetts where thousands of convicted sex offenders have been assigned the lowest possible "level one" status, which means they are not listed on any public registries, even though they were convicted of sex crimes against children. In most other states, abusing a child is a per se high-risk offense, and the public has a right to know everything.

And let's *get rid of the confusing language* in sex crimes laws. Why can't all states agree to have only two crimes: "Child rape" and "non-penetrating sexual abuse." These will cover about 99 percent of sex crimes against children. The use of only two terms, instead of thirty, will make it a whole lot easier for officials in Virginia (for example) to figure out what to do with a registered sex offender who moved there after being convicted in Alabama. Under the current system, Virginia officials have to call officials in Alabama to ask: *"What exactly do you guys mean by level three molestation?"* While cops are making phone calls to figure out who they're dealing with, the guy they're worried about is already making his moves on another child.

It would also help if every state determined an offender's "dangerousness" *before* sentencing, rather than the way it's done now, which is either after the guy is released from prison, or at best, just before. This is absurd. We have a much better chance of making the correct determination about whether a predator will offend again if we test him right after the crime is committed. This is the moment when information about his life in the real world is fresh and is being assessed by criminal justice experts like probation officers, judges, and prosecutors. Making a decision about "dangerousness" ten years later, when he's on his way out of prison, is silly because his lawyer will argue that he's no longer a threat to children given that he hasn't committed any "new" offenses in ten years. The obvious response is "of *course* the guy hasn't committed any new offenses in ten years. There aren't any children living in his cellblock!" But why even enable such a dopey argument to begin with?

It's economically efficient to assess dangerousness when a judge is also figuring out an appropriate punishment. Simply put, the court system saves money by examining one set of facts to answer two legal questions at the same time.

Let's air this scenario out a little bit. If a perpetrator is dangerous when he's on his way *in* to prison, he should bear the burden of proving that he is no longer dangerous when he's on his way *out*. When perpetrators realize they have to overcome a dangerousness ruling against them, they might actually spend time in prison engaged in meaningful counseling, trying to redeem themselves and *earn* their way out from under the "dangerous" label. The current model in many states has it exactly backwards. It presumes that even super-predators are safe by putting the burden on the government to prove dangerousness long after the crime, and long after the guy has spent years behind bars.

Some say we shouldn't even have dangerousness hearings because we can't really predict dangerousness, and I agree we can't do it with precision. But we can make pretty good judgments. And remember, some of the same people who say we can't predict a criminal's future behavior by looking at his past behavior claim that the mother of the victim in Michael Jackson's trial had no credibility because she lied in the past to receive welfare benefits. Jackson's lawyers argued that the jury should disbelieve the mother about Jackson's abuse because by lying in the past, she was generally "more inclined to lie."

Note that they made the exact *opposite* argument about whether the jury should hear evidence about Jackson's past abuse of kids to determine whether he was "more inclined" to abuse kids in general.

Defense lawyers can't have it both ways. Either bad behavior in the past is evidence of likely future behavior, or it isn't. It can't only be a reliable predictor when the rule is applied to victims.

In fact, the rule should apply *more* often to sex offenders than to people who lied to welfare officials because the data often show that the average sex offender has scores of victims under his belt before he gets caught the first time. We also know that a large percentage of offenders are simply unstoppable. (I chose that word carefully. I don't want to say "incurable" because that would imply that raping children is an illness. It isn't. It's a choice.)

Defense attorneys often cite "federal studies" and claim, falsely, that recidivism rates are low for sex offenders. They conveniently forget to mention, however, that federal researchers measure *arrest* rates, not *incidence* rates - a crucial distinction given that 90 percent of child sex assaults are never reported, much less prosecuted.

Rather than representing any sort of good news, those federal studies may well indicate that perpetrators are committing far more offenses than ever before, but they're evading capture because after going to prison the first time, they figured out how to get better at silencing their victims through more effective tactics, such as using drugs that cause victims to suffer amnesia during the crime.

Because we have the ability to identify individuals who are highly likely to commit sex crimes, it's dumb to say a convicted sex offender should get a clean slate when he leaves prison, and that he "paid his debt" to society. The underlying premise of such a claim is that the guy paid a sufficient "debt." In a study of child sex abuse prosecutions in Rhode Island, researchers found that the average punishment was probation. That's right – no jail time at all!

Even if we could find a case where a particular perpetrator truly did "pay his debt" with an appropriately long sentence of incarceration, it wouldn't mean that he's safe to be around children. Paying one's debt does not ensure one's safety to be around children, and if a guy is *not* safe, there's nothing wrong with taking reasonable steps to restrain him from offending again.

While it's also true that we shouldn't assume people without criminal records *are* safe, the fact that we can't identify all dangerous criminals with precision is no excuse not to do the best we can about the ones we *do* know.

The Constitution promises no person a blank slate after a criminal conviction, and though everyone deserves a shot at redemption, it should be *earned*, not handed over arbitrarily to an obviously dangerous criminal who has no remorse and every intention of offending again. But we do it all the time, in every state, and these guys are living in *your* neighborhood.

We need the media to help hold public officials responsible when they release dangerous offenders into our communities without effective monitoring and oversight. The media are pretty good at putting horrible crimes on the front page *after* they happen, but there's not enough attention to the bad guys *before* they pounce.

There are exceptions, as when the *Boston Globe* hammered the Catholic Church about the priest sex-abuse scandal, and included information about dangerous perpetrators who were still actively employed as priests. Many of the priests hadn't offended against a child in decades, and had never been convicted of a crime, but the Globe released information about them so that parents could protect their children from harm. All newspapers should provide similar coverage about offenders *other than priests*, even if they haven't committed any new offenses in a long time.

Political leaders need to be more proactive, too. Elected officials jump like new puppies to get their faces on the news after disaster strikes, but they're nowhere to be found *before* horrible things happen. This reactionary approach to lawmaking requires too many innocent people to suffer before meaningful laws are enacted.

It's particularly awful in states like Massachusetts where defense attorneys control the legislature and rarely do right by victims. Sex crimes generally don't register high on the list of either major political party. Too many conservatives think the government should be out of the business of "personal" crimes. And traditional liberals think that locking up criminals is offensive to individual liberty. Libertarians don't help because they see all government power as bad for freedom, and all sexual activity as good for the individual.

No politician is openly "pro rape," of course, and while conservatives tend to be more willing to speak up for crime victims than liberals, we're in desperate need of a whole new party; one that puts civility ahead of all special interests. Forget Democrats, Republicans, Independents and even the "Green Party." We need an "Anti-Violence Party," fast!

In the meantime, with a vacuum in political leadership we need *nonpartisan* leadership in media. Before Bill O'Reilly took on the task of fighting for tougher laws against sex offenders, nobody gave a damn about kids. Like me, O'Reilly cares more about kids than partisan allegiance, so he supports ideas that make sense, no matter how the Republicans or Democrats feel about it. We need more of this independent spirit on every network and in every newspaper.

It would also help if every state would get around to eliminating the statute of limitations for all sex crimes, but especially sex crimes against children. When kids are victimized they know it doesn't feel right, but because they haven't reached sexual maturity, they don't understand the magnitude of what's happening. And because they have no power to do anything about it, they develop psychological coping skills that help them avoid the emotional pain. In the short term, this is generally a good thing, because it enables abused children to function in their day-to-day lives without decompensating. But it's *not* good for kids in the long run because when they become adults, they still have all that suffering inside.

Well-known trauma doctor Bessell van der Kolk, MD, calls this the "Body Keeping Score." In his work looking at the brains of traumatized children, he tracks the way trauma happens, and how it stays in victims' bodies and minds even though they may have no conscious "narrative" memory of the abuse. When kids are old enough to understand what happened, they often seek therapy to try to fix that childhood pain, but the brain that learned to cope all those years ago doesn't exist anymore, so the repair work isn't easy. And the delay in awareness and understanding makes it's tough for an adult survivor of child abuse to ever appreciate the causal connection between his adult suffering and abuse that ended many years earlier.

Another noted doctor and researcher, Vincent Felitti, MD, has documented countless stories from adults who suffered terrible experiences as children, only to have that suffering continue to wreak havoc throughout the victims' lives, often manifesting as serious health consequences in adulthood. Felitti's work on the ACE (Adverse Childhood Experience) study along with van der Kolk's work on trauma and the brain, emphasize that the very nature of childhood renders many victims incapable of dealing with or even understanding their pain while the abuse is occurring.

As adults, victims can begin to process information about what happened to them as children, but they're never really "cured," which is why it's so cruel to have any limitation on the time frame within which victims can seek justice. And because abuse is tougher on some kids than others, it's wrong to have a limitation period that arbitrarily cuts off access to justice when victims can't help the circumstances that inhibited faster healing.

Child predators understand that in many states, the statute of limitations runs out for kids long before they even figure out they're in pain, which is one of the reasons they choose kids as victims. Right about the time a child is finally capable of talking to cops or filing a lawsuit, the courtroom door slams shut.

Perpetrators who know they can walk away from a crime scot-free when the clock runs out are often extra cruel to their victims. They want to make sure kids stay quiet a good long time. Defense attorneys and like-minded lawmakers don't care. They complain that eliminating limitation periods is unconstitutional even though there's no such thing as a Constitutional right to run out the clock. That's why they call it a "statute" of limitations - it has nothing to do with the Constitution.

If the accused can't get a fair trial in a criminal case because too much time has passed, he can file a motion explaining why the case should be dismissed. And if a victim takes advantage of the long time period to file a fraudulent civil case, he or she should be sanctioned and the lawsuit dismissed. But no decent person can argue with a straight face that the monsters who pick on kids should not *at least* spend the rest of their lives looking over their shoulders, worried that they might be brought to justice. Making the bums nervous is the least we can do.

While we're on the topic of lawmaking, let's talk about the silliness of some legislators who whine about sex offender registries being harmful and inhumane because they stigmatize rapists and make them feel bad about themselves. Of *course* they do! But many defense attorneys say that registries are unfair, and that the rap sheets of convicted child predators should be protected by *privacy rights* laws, so that perpetrators don't feel ashamed of themselves.

Stealing for a moment the signature phrase of my deceased pal, investigative journalist Dominick Dunne, *I find that odd*.

It takes a lot of gall to insist that the conviction record of any sex offender should be shielded by "privacy" rights. We're talking about people who were prosecuted with *public* dollars in a *public* courtroom by *public* officials. If a mother of a victim wants to tell all her friends about what the guy did, or if she wants to talk about it on television, write a book, or post it on the Internet, there is nothing anyone can do to stop her, because there's nothing private about a criminal activity.

But in virtually every state, when people want to put this public information in an efficient, accessible, and user-friendly public place such as a registry, the ACLU, the criminal defense bar and radical liberals start yelling about how identifying sex offenders in public is a violation of "privacy" rights. These are the same groups that then line the pockets of lawmakers in charge of key committees, such as "Criminal Justice," "Judiciary," and "Third Reading," that make crucial decisions about laws that affect the rights of sex offenders. It's an incestuous pigsty.

In Massachusetts, this sort of nonsense forestalled the enactment of a registry law for years. (In fact, we were the last state in the nation to have one.) We finally got a bill through, and then the public defenders' office used *our tax dollars* to file multiple lawsuits to prevent the registry law from being enforced.

The public clearly wanted a sex offender registry but the unholy alliance of the ACLU and the criminal defense bar stopped the law from becoming a reality for years. When that effort eventually failed, and the registry was finally up and running, the public defenders' office then used *more* public money to inhibit the registry from functioning at full force. Unbelievable!!

In Massachusetts, where we really can't love our sex offenders enough, is it any wonder we elected Deval Patrick to be our governor, even though Patrick called a convicted rapist "thoughtful" after he brutally attacked an elderly woman in her own home and left her for dead. Seriously! A man named Ben LaGuer viciously raped a grandmother for eight hours, and nearly killed her by strangling her with a phone cord.

A jury found LaGuer guilty, though LaGuer refused to accept responsibility for his crime or express any remorse. DNA tests years later confirmed LaGuer's guilt, *after which,* Governor Patrick not only called the guy "thoughtful," he recommended LaGuer for parole. If you were a rapist, wouldn't you want to live in Massachusetts?

We clearly have a long way to go in Massachusetts and in many other states. For now, here's my message to people like Deval Patrick: We're watching. And we notice when you say and do things to elevate the interests of dangerous criminals over the safety of innocent, law-abiding citizens.

So knock it off and try listening to the people for a change. We have enough problems without having to figure out why our governor thinks a vicious rapist is "thoughtful." What if Ben LaGuer raped one of your two daughters, Governor Patrick? Would the guy still be "thoughtful"?

EIGHTEEN

Calling Child Pornography Harmless

When a forty-two year-old teacher on Cape Cod named David Berglund was arrested in the Fall of 2006 on child pornography charges, the feds announced that they had found more than ten thousand illegal images of abused children on his computer.

Don't let your eyes slide over that number - *ten thousand*. This is an enormous number. Have you ever sent a couple of hundred invitations for a wedding or stuffed five hundred letters in a political campaign? Ten thousand is a lot of anything, and the idea that one person could have so many pictures of little kids being sexually violated seems almost incomprehensible.

But in the world of child pornography, numbers like that are not uncommon. Exploiting children is the kind of crime that fuels a demand for more, which is why cops rarely find one, or two, or even only a few dozen images on a perpetrator's computer. But this doesn't stop defense attorneys from talking about child pornography as if it's a victimless crime, or some kind of edgy art. "He's not a dangerous pervert," they claim. He's "eccentric" and "misunderstood."

Sure he is.

A few of Berglund's photos were described in court as depicting little boys in frontal nudity, lying on beds, and sexually assaulting each other. News reports said other pictures showed children victimized by bondage and whips. But defense attorneys still got away with soft-peddling the stuff because the photographs themselves could not be shown to the public. It's the ultimate dirty trick, isn't it? Defense attorneys can claim the pictures aren't that bad, and they get away with lying about it, because they know there's no way for police or prosecutors to prove otherwise to the public.

Bill O'Reilly featured the Berglund story soon after it broke. He had me and Berglund's lawyer on his show to talk about the story during a special edition of the *O'Reilly Factor* in front of a live audience in Boston in 2006, as part of the Fox News Channel's tenth-anniversary special. In my view, O'Reilly deserves an Emmy for the restraint he demonstrated in not punching Berglund's lawyer, Jeffrey Nathan, after Nathan said that ninety days behind bars would be enough punishment because his client didn't hurt any children.

Excuse me?!

Never mind that Nathan undercut his own client's presumption of innocence by talking about what kind of punishment his client deserved before he had a chance for a trial, Nathan said he didn't see how the pictures caused harm to children. And then he made the even more despicable claim that it wasn't such a bad crime because the victims were from other countries.

I was sitting right next to the guy when he added the shocker about kids from other countries. I'm glad I didn't have a baseball bat close at hand at that moment, because I would have been sorely tempted to whack him upside the head. Bill started yelling at the guy, and my murderous moment passed. But the truly weird thing was that a few people in the audience seemed to be cheering for Nathan, which suggests that some of my fellow residents of Massachusetts are either in the child-porn business or are desperately out of touch with reality.

The epidemic of child pornography is seriously out of control, and it's destroying the lives of real children. (I don't care where in the world those poor children live.) And yet the crime is often punished on a par with shoplifting, largely because most of us have never seen the stuff, which makes it harder to argue with specificity about why it's so horrible, or hold prosecutors and judges accountable when they give out lenient sentences. In turn, guys like Nathan can claim with a straight face that child pornography is no big deal.

It isn't even necessarily a felony in California and a few other states, including Colorado, Oregon, and North Dakota. But even in a federal court, or in a state where possession of child porn *is* a felony, a guy like Berglund typically faces no more than ten years in prison. Let's do the math to understand how silly that is. If each of the ten thousand images depicted a different victim, that's less than a day behind bars for each child. And even if many pictures show the same child, do we really want to give these types of criminals volume discounts for abusing one child repeatedly?

The Internet has facilitated unprecedented growth, organizational strength, and even political clout in the child-porn industry. These factors are moving us in the wrong direction.

It's outrageous to argue that child pornography doesn't hurt real children when research shows that demand for the stuff creates the industry, and that new material is necessary to make sure demand doesn't dry up. Research also shows that almost all child rapists use child pornography, either to normalize the behavior for the victim, or to "teach" the child how to behave. Similarly, almost all users of child pornography also sexually abuse kids. To me, this shows an obvious connection between the possession of photographs and the physical act of abusing a child.

In his testimony before Congress in 2002, Michael J. Heimbach, head of the FBI's Crimes Against Children Unit, cited the Hernandez Study (2000) in which Dr. Andres E. Hernandez, in his capacity as the director of a Federal Sex Offender Treatment Program, found that two-thirds of federal prisoners incarcerated on child-pornography charges had also molested children. Even more shocking, the prisoners reported having sexually assaulted an average of more than *thirty children each* without ever having been detected. In another study, published in the *Journal of Abnormal Psychology* in August 2006, researchers found that using child pornography is a stronger predictor of child-sexual abuse than whether a person was previously convicted of a sexual crime against a child. Think about that. A person who uses child porn is even *more dangerous* to children than a convicted child rapist!

Can we all just agree, conclusively, that it is unacceptably dangerous to allow users of child pornography to be anywhere near children? And can we also agree that users have to be held just as accountable as child rapists, not only because they represent the demand side but also because users tend to become producers?

As Attorney General Gonzales explained in his testimony to Congress, when users become desensitized to certain photographs, they want something new and different, such as more violent images, but in order to gain access to new material, they have to produce their own photos of new kids.

Against this powerful evidence, some argue that too much government intervention in the fight against child porn threatens First Amendment principles even though the United States Supreme Court long ago ruled that child pornography has no Constitutional protection. But unless you've seen the stuff, you can't know how ridiculous the argument really is. Most of us have no context to visualize a child being raped, which is one of the reasons I try to be more graphic than most when I write about the issue. I want people to understand how awful it is, which won't happen if we keep saying "photos of children being abused" or "naked photos of kids."

Let's agree to be blunt from now on. It might not work in polite company, but it's important if we're going to help keep kids safe. Child pornography is never an airbrushed photo of a little boy on the beach with his rear end showing. Never. According to a 2005 study funded by Congress, 80 percent of child pornography depicts children being penetrated, which is what you would think of as rape or sodomy. A full 21 percent *also* involves sadism such as bondage, whips, chains, and ligatures wrapped around little arms, legs, and necks while body parts and objects are inserted into tiny private areas. Something like 83 percent of child pornography depicts children between ages six and twelve and only one percent consists of images of simple child nudity - the stuff some people claim is "art." Sadly, and maybe most disturbing, Attorney General Gonzales says it's often parents of the victims taking the pictures, as we saw with Justin Berry, the young man who told Congress in 2006 that he was pimped by his father who made him engage in sex acts for money via a Webcam from his home.

Justin Berry's story brought tough, cynical old member of Congress to tears. Most hadn't heard anything so shocking and all were distraught to learn that at any given moment, more than fifty thousand people are lurking on the Internet, hunting for children to exploit and rape for profit. The fact that smart members of Congress were so uninformed on the issue is powerful evidence that we have a lot of work to do.

Child pornography is a multibillion-dollar business run by people who know that law enforcement will never have enough resources to stop them completely. This is why we need more public/private partnerships, like NBC's "To Catch a Predator" program. The wealth of a major network helps to stretch law enforcement's budget. But money alone will never do the trick because pornographers know the ACLU and others will spend even more money defending child porn by waving the flag around.

The ACLU has done some very important work, especially when it comes to protecting subversive political speech. But consider that the former president of the Virginia chapter of the ACLU was arrested in 2007 on child porn charges. Charles Rust Tierney allegedly subscribed to hard-core websites over a period of years. This is a guy who, on behalf of the ACLU in Virginia, successfully fought against the use of filters that would have stopped people from accessing child pornography on computers in public libraries. ACLU chapters around the country have also:

1) Filed lawsuits opposing sex offender registries;

2) Challenged laws that require sex predators to stay away from schools, parks, day care centers, and libraries;

3) Opposed mandatory minimum sentences for child rapists;

4) Provided free legal services to NAMBLA; an organization that advocates against laws that forbid adults to have sex with children;

5) Argued in court that the rape of a fourteen-year-old boy by an adult was not a crime, in part because teenagers have a Constitutional right to be "free from state compulsion" when making personal decisions about sexual activity.

Here's my prescription for the ACLU: Take a vacation from protecting child predators for a while, and fight to protect *children's freedoms* for a change. Even the densest member of the ACLU can understand the downside of slavery, which is exactly what it's called when kids are used as sex objects for profit. Someone needs to tell the

ACLU they should worry *more* about ordinary people abusing children than about the government power that hopefully, one day, will bring them down.

Until then, we can all help protect kids by paying more attention to the warning signs that indicate a child is being abused. When the scandal involving Representative Mark Foley broke in 2006, his congressional colleagues fell all over themselves trying to explain why a sexually explicit e-mail wasn't enough to prove that Foley was dangerous. But there were many other red flags that should have given even a mildly explicit email more significance. Foley was inappropriate with congressional pages for a long time - well before the guy was bold and stupid enough to put his intentions in writing.

Foley's foolishness notwithstanding, most perpetrators don't send damning emails, which is why parents, Congressmen and others responsible for the well-being of children have a responsibility to learn what red flags look like and not wait for the perpetrators to reveal their crimes.

For example, people who prey on kids often display an unusual interest in young people and usually have only a few close friends of their own age. They're typically narcissistic and naive, and they often behave in ways that disrespect boundaries in interpersonal relationships.

Contrary to popular myth, child predators are not typically gay. Most child-sex offenses are male-on-female, and although some offenders are homosexual in orientation (the loathsome group NAMBLA was formed specifically to advance the interests of such offenders) for the most part, even homosexual child pornography has nothing to do with being gay. So don't let people like Mark Foley (who tried to win sympathy points by announcing he was gay when his scandal became public) fool you. When a child is victimized by an adult, nobody cares that the attacker might be gay. The only thing that matters is that the victim is a child.

It also matters that predators are very good at selecting kids they know they can control. As renowned expert Dr. Anna Salter writes in her book, *Predators*, child sex abusers often test the waters with a potential victim before they pounce by grooming them and seeing how they react to relatively benign behavior. They might use inappropriate language or touch a child's leg, and if the victim doesn't protest, they'll go further.

To ensure that a child doesn't tell, a perpetrator might invite a child to participate in illicit behavior, such as looking at pornography, drinking alcohol or smoking pot. For teenage victims, access to illicit material can be exciting, and because they know their parents will disapprove, they keep it a secret. Then, when the sexual abuse starts happening, the child doesn't say anything because he's worried about getting into trouble for using drugs or alcohol.

Not all perpetrators groom their victims, and not all kids show signs that they're being harmed. Sometimes kids really like the extra attention, even though they hate the abuse - especially when the attention is coming from someone important in their lives. Kids get confused about feeling good and bad at the same time, so they stay quiet. They feel partly responsible, as if they deserve the abuse or owe the perp a little sex in exchange for all the attention, favorable treatment and access to illicit goodies.

Child abusers are easy to spot so long as the people responsible for protecting kids know what they're looking for. All too often, though, when a child is getting special attention from a relative or other trusted adult, it goes unnoticed because it looks on the outside like innocent generosity, and sometimes it is. But until we start questioning whether an adult's unnecessarily kind behavior toward a child might be too good to be true, the pornographers and sex predators will continue to prey on children, undetected.

Fixing the problem is all about keeping the forest in sight, even as you're looking at trees. This means scrutinizing e-mails and text messages and Facebook pages to see who's talking to our children, and asking tough questions that might make us and our kids uncomfortable. We have no choice, because if we do nothing until there's a smoking gun, it will be too late. Stopping perpetrators means getting involved *before* the abuse starts, even if it means putting a stop to a relationship that would never have become abusive. You know the old saying, "Better safe than sorry." Our kids won't like it when we intrude into their relationships, but that's O.K. They don't need us to be their buddies, they need us to help them make good choices. We can't afford to wait until the smoke turns into a fire, because by then, our kids will have been burned.

Finally, we have to be more honest with ourselves. It's easy to turn a blind eye to the warning signs that indicate our kids are in trouble. It feels a whole lot better to pretend there's nothing wrong because no parent wants to believe their child is being sexually abused or exploited. But this head-in-the-sand approach is terribly dangerous to kids. Let's give up a little bit of that urge to feel good all the time and open our eyes to the more painful truth about the monster in our midst. He's waiting to snatch his next victim the minute we look away.

NINETEEN

Inventing Imaginary Constitutional Rights

We've all heard of Miranda warnings and Miranda rights. They're important because they protect all of us from unjust government power at the hands of law enforcement officials. And though the law has long been settled that not every Miranda violation requires the beheading of a police officer or the elevation of a murderer to sainthood, try telling that to defense attorneys who believe that everything cops do wrong during an interrogation, whether intentionally or by mistake, or whether there is a major or minor infraction, is akin to a federal crime.

Miranda rights weren't even technically Constitutional rights until recently. When Miranda was decided in 1966, the Supreme Court wrote at length about the importance of having police advise suspects in their custody that they had the right to remain silent. This would help protect the Fifth Amendment to the U.S. Constitution, which guarantees freedom from coerced confessions.

But the Court did not rule that Miranda warnings were Constitutionally *mandatory*. They said it was a good idea, adding that Congress had authority to enact legislation to propose a different way of protecting Fifth Amendment rights. Thereafter, Congress passed a new federal law providing that police should advise suspects of their Fifth Amendment rights, but if they didn't, it was not necessarily a Constitutional violation. The new law provided that all the circumstances of a suspect's confession should be examined to determine whether the confession was coerced. Failure to give a Miranda warning would be an important factor, but it would not be enough, alone, to prove that a suspect's Constitutional rights were violated.

More recently, the Supreme Court had a chance to decide whether Congress' proposal was good enough, or whether the time had come to elevate the 1966 Miranda decision to a Constitutional mandate. The Court chose the latter option and Miranda warnings are now Constitutionally required.

Most people saw the Court's new ruling as a good thing because nobody wants cops forcing or torturing people to confess. I'll be the first one to unlock the jail cell and let a guilty guy go free if a cop beats the hell out of a guy to make him admit his guilt. In a healthy democracy, restraints on unjust government power are a good thing.

But when every Miranda violation, no matter how minor, becomes the means by which defense attorneys demand ridiculous remedies, such as dismissal of murder charges and million-dollar lawsuits, we're all in deep trouble.

Just as calling child pornography art demeans the First Amendment, calling every technical Miranda violation a profound insult to freedom diminishes the stature of the Fifth Amendment, and trivializes serious Constitutional violations.

Yet this is exactly what some defense attorney pundits were clamoring for during the 2006 prosecution of John Couey for the brutal rape and murder of little Jessica Lunsford. Lawyers for Couey had asked the judge to throw out Couey's entire confession because it had been obtained in violation of his Miranda rights. Most observers, like me, said things like, "Well, it might be appropriate to throw out his confession but that's O.K. because there's plenty of evidence left over to prove the guy's guilt." A group of defense lawyers, however, argued that all the evidence should be thrown out, including the discovery of little Jessica's body. The child was found buried in Couey's back yard, hugging a stuffed animal. Forensic experts said she'd been buried alive and left to suffocate to death. Defense lawyers didn't care. They wanted the whole case dismissed to punish the cops for asking Couey questions after he said the word "lawyer."

Think about that. Defense lawyers wanted a confessed child murderer to walk away scot-free just to punish the cops. Forget about the harm to society, especially defenseless kids, defense lawyers wanted Couey set free so he could start hunting for his next victim.

This is an increasingly common and disturbing attitude in our criminal justice system, and it's time to put the brakes on, or at least have a conversation about whether we're imposing too much on the freedom of *innocent* people to indulge the wild-eyed demands of defense attorneys.

The framers would not be pleased.

The media should help out here. While the accused generally (though not always) has stronger Constitutional rights in a criminal courtroom, compared to the rights of victims, the media functions in the real world. And in the real world, sometimes the victim has Constitutional rights at stake, too, and sometimes the public interest is paramount to wholly contrived claims of a defense attorney that an accused has Constitutional rights at stake.

This means that when a defense attorney makes a nonsensical claim about due process rights, or dumps false or irrelevant information about a victim into a judicial proceeding, the media should resist publishing the nonsense until a judge agrees with the defense arguments about due process, or determines that evidence about a victim is both true and relevant. This will protect the jury from believing things that aren't true about the Constitution and the evidence.

This wouldn't mean defendants don't get a fair shake. It would mean victims don't get an unfair shake. Judges and the media should take steps to ensure that jurors render verdicts based on the evidence they hear during trial, not defense-produced information that was published outside the courtroom.

Defense attorneys have to do their part, too, by resisting the urge to insist that all the bad things that happen to accused criminals are Constitutional violations, and all the bad things they do to victims during the investigation and trial are constitutionally authorized. If they don't scale back, the defense bar can be sure that victims and their lawyers will be fighting harder and harder to challenge their excesses in the real courtroom and in the court of public opinion.

For example, criminal lawyers often argue that it violates the accused's Constitutional rights for a police officer to wear his uniform to trial. Why? Because the jury will be biased in favor of a man in uniform. But if a defense attorney is representing a priest accused of child rape, he will become indignant at the idea that a priest shouldn't be allowed to wear his collar in court because the priest has a Constitutional right to practice his religion during his testimony. Oh, please! The Constitution is hardly so fickle.

I can only guess what's coming next. Will it be criminal lawyers demanding that a case be dismissed to punish a prosecutor for smiling at a child? Will they insist that the Constitution allows a rapist to inspect a victim's bedroom closet to look for evidence? How about inspecting her genitals? The Supreme Court of Appeals for the State of West Virginia ruled recently that a child rape victim could be ordered to submit to a penetrating vaginal examination at the request of her attacker during a rape trial. Think about that. A judge presiding over a child rape trial ordered the *rape* of a child rape victim and the state's highest court *upheld the decision*. What is in the water in West Virginia?

It's unconstitutional, of course, to order the rape of a child in the name of justice, but none of the appellate justices seemed to care.

What happens when a victim refuses to submit to court-ordered rape? Should she be held down? Sent to jail? What country is this anyway? Did the judge think the state of West Virginia had been moved to the Middle East?

Another idiot judge threatened to throw a rape victim named Tori Bowen in jail in 2007 when she refused to obey his asinine demand that she not use the words "rape" or "sexual assault" during her testimony. Nebraska Judge Jeffre Cheuvront said she could call it "sex" but not "rape." He also ordered her not to call herself a "victim" and said she should refer to the "sexual assault kit" as the "sexual kit." There were other nutty demands, too. When I heard about the case, I flew to Nebraska to represent her, for free.

I teamed up with local counsel and filed all the right papers to allow me to practice law in Nebraska for that particular case, and then I filed a brief explaining to the judge he had no authority to dictate the words a victim can use to describe her own victimization.

Cheuvront was furious that I proved him to be a fool. He ignored me for days and wouldn't even have a hearing on my motion. He waited until I was on a plane back to Boston before making my client take the stand to tell him whether she intended to obey his order during trial. I'd prepared her well and anticipated that the cowardly judge would make her take the stand only after I left town. She looked straight at him and said: "Your Honor, when I raise my hand and swear to tell the truth, the whole truth and nothing but the truth, that's exactly what I intend to do." She was great.

The judge stormed off the bench, miffed that Tori wouldn't agree to obey his dopey order. He was so angry, he dismissed the charges, claiming that there had been too much negative publicity after the group PAVE had protesters show up near the courthouse with their mouths covered in duct tape, carrying signs that criticized Cheuvront's order as foolish.

The prosecutor agreed to refile the charges and while we waited for the case to start up again, I filed a lawsuit against Judge Cheuvront in Nebraska federal court to stop him from issuing another order against Tori after the case was refiled.

The federal court was not thrilled that a sassy female lawyer from Boston had the audacity to file a federal lawsuit against a state court judge in Nebraska, but they knew I was right. So although the court slammed me in its ruling for being audacious, they also dropped a footnote saying that forbidding a rape victim to use the word rape during a rape trial was reminiscent of the kinds of things one hears about from countries where women wear burkas.

In other words, even though the federal court didn't like the fact that I'd sued a state court judge, they thought Judge Cheuvront was a dope.

Not long thereafter, Judge Cheuvront was embarrassed again when a prestigious First Amendment watchdog organization gave him their annual "Muzzle Award." The Thomas Jefferson Center for Free Expression gives out the annual prize to individuals and organizations that engage in "particularly egregious or ridiculous affronts" to First Amendment rights.

Cheuvront's stupidity was outdone only by the antics of a weirdo state senator from Nebraska who filed a federal lawsuit against God to mock the case I'd filed against Cheuvront. The senator said at the time, "If a rape victim can sue a judge, then I can sue God." You can't make this stuff up. I think the court is still waiting for the whacky senator to take God's deposition.

In an even more shocking case, disabled sexual assault victim Ruby McDonough was brought to tears in a Massachusetts courtroom by a defense attorney who claimed he was merely protecting his client's Constitutional rights when he mocked her language disability.

Ruby had suffered a stroke years earlier, which landed her in a nursing home struggling with physical disabilities and a disorder called aphasia. She understood everything that was going on around her, but she couldn't communicate by using narrative language. When an aide at the nursing home named Kofi Agana was arrested for sexually abusing Ruby in her bed, Agana's lawyer demanded that Ruby be forbidden to testify on the grounds that she was "incompetent" because she could not speak in full sentences.

Ruby could say things like "yes" and "no," and she could use her good arm to point at things, but she couldn't describe in narrative style the disgusting thing Agana did to her body.

The judge held a competency hearing, during which Agana's lawyer was allowed to ask Ruby things like "can you tell us what happened?" Of course, Ruby couldn't respond, and the lawyer continued to exploit her disabilities as Ruby struggled in frustration. To really dig the knife in deep, Agana's lawyer stood in front of Ruby to block her view of Agana, then asked, "Do you see the man who assaulted you in the courtroom?"

Ruby couldn't say yes because the jerk was blocking her view. But she also couldn't say, "No," because she knew Agana was there. She started crying. Nobody said a word. Nobody objected to say that the lawyer was violating Ruby's rights as a disabled person. The prosecutor, the judge, and even Ruby's advocate stayed silent.

The judge found Ruby incompetent because she couldn't narrate her testimony. That's when I got the call to represent her.

I filed an appeal for Ruby, accusing everyone in the room of violating Ruby's rights under the Americans With Disabilities Act. I also accused the attorney from a victims' rights law center group in Boston of committing legal malpractice for doing nothing to protect Ruby's rights.

Our appeal was successful and Ruby had her day in court, where she had another chance to identify Agana. Again the defense attorney tried to block Ruby's view, but this time Ruby didn't cry, and she didn't even need me to object, though I was ready. Ruby waved her good arm back and forth, repeatedly, motioning the lawyer to get out of her way. When he finally stepped back, Ruby jabbed a pointed finger at Agana, and firmly testified, "Yes, yes yes!"

Ruby's appeal was a landmark ruling for the entire country because it was the first time any appellate court had ever addressed the rights of disabled crime victims to *participate and communicate* effectively in criminal trials, with the help of all necessary accommodations and assistive devices.

Other courts had ruled that wheelchair ramps should be installed so that disabled people could get *in* to the courthouse, but until Ruby's case, no court had ever addressed what happens when a crime victim's disabilities make it hard to provide testimony after they make it *in* to the courtroom. The ruling is good news for all people with disabilities.

Most importantly, Ruby's case forbids defense attorneys to mock or exploit a victim's disabilities in court. If they ever *try* to pull the stunts that Agana's lawyer pulled, they can be sued for a lot of money, and the judge can get in trouble, too, for allowing it to happen.

If Ruby McDonough can change the criminal justice system, you can, too. Each of us has to do whatever we can to make sure that those who have been harmed by criminal violence are not then compelled to submit to even more degradation in the name of justice.

TWENTY

Launching Political Persecutions

I hope that by now you've picked up on a theme that
I have unapologetically injected into many chapters of this
book: I'm as mean as it gets when it comes to criminals.

I'm sick of hearing how punishment is vengeance,
imprisonment does no good, and all the rest of the addle-
brained nonsense that emerges from judges on the bench
and from defense attorneys who prop themselves up on the
front steps of courthouses, with cameras rolling as they
whine about how jails are bad, punishment is fascism, blah,
blah, blah.

Punishment works. The research is clear that when
punishment is swift and harsh, bad behavior is diminished.
Studies also show that when law-abiding citizens perceive
that the justice system does not work as it should, people
will stop reporting crime and will refuse to participate in the
legal process. The inevitable next step is social chaos.

That's why when judges go soft on the bad guys out
of some twisted allegiance to the idea that thugs need hugs,
my arms start flailing, and I get really steamed. When
someone tries to defend their position by saying something
stupid like, "We don't have enough prison space to lock up

all the child predators," I'm ready to scream. If we really don't have enough jail cells for the dangerous criminals, what the hell were we doing wasting a bed on Martha Stewart for nine months?

I know she lied to SEC investigators, and lying is wrong. But federal prosecutors who went after Martha Stewart spent way too much of the public's money sending a liar to prison. Suppose there had been only one bed left for a female criminal. Who would you rather see in it? Martha, or one of the umpteen teachers who perpetrate sex crimes against their students - teachers who rarely see a single day, much less nine months, behind bars?

What did we really accomplish by sending Martha Stewart to jail, anyway?

I realize it's important to send a message, even with nonviolent crime, when the goal is to prevent similar misconduct in the future. But didn't Martha get that message loud and clear when she was forced to resign from her company, take a huge financial hit, and was then indicted on the world stage? Sure, pounding a criminal a little extra sometimes makes sense if you're trying to set an example for others. But message-sending can be carried too far, and when prosecutors go overboard, demanding incarceration and making a small case seem like the most important prosecution since the Scopes Trial, the backlash can nullify the intended message. Even worse, as in Stewart's case, it can breed cynicism and contempt for the entire system. How long will the public believe in a system that can't seem to get its priorities straight?

It was clear from the beginning that the feds latched on to Martha Stewart because prosecutors get a lot of public attention when they go after a celebrity. As messages go, the feds get a lot of bang for their (taxpayer) buck when millions of people watch a case unfold.

By whacking around a big cheese like Stewart, the feds probably thought they were giving us renewed confidence in the integrity of the stock market and that our future investments would be safe because prosecutors were finally getting tough on corporate criminals.

But let's be honest: There never would have been a prosecution if Martha Stewart had been a nobody, or if Stewart had been Kelly Ripa. Suppose Ripa had gotten the same stock tip from Martha's friend Sam Waksal, and let's say she thanked him on her show for the heads-up about the impending implosion of Waksal's company. Would Kelly Ripa have been prosecuted? No way. She's too beloved. The same goes for Bill Cosby, Julie Andrews, and anyone who even looks a little bit like Jimmy Stewart.

Our secular saints (including valuable athletes) are rarely held accountable because the feds raise a wet finger to the wind before deciding whether it's worth it to have angry mobs of fans in the streets. It would be terrible for public relations, which would then affect the outcome of the next presidential election because United States Attorneys are appointed by the President. Sure, there might have been a fine for someone like Kelly Ripa, a hand slap, community service, and so on; but there would have been no protracted prosecution, and no politically unpalatable prison time.

But prosecutors easily get away with going after an over-the-top prosecution of a "bitchy" woman who made it big in a man's world. Why? Because when the wet finger gets raised on a mean character like Martha Stewart, the wind doesn't blow. There's no political downside to going after a hugely successful businesswoman with a reputation for behaving badly and apologizing to nobody on her way up the ladder of success. The prosecutors knew they could use Martha as a whipping girl because she was disliked by a large enough segment of the population. Forget that other CEOs who had ruined lives and decimated retirement funds were still walking the streets. People would pay attention to and applaud the Martha-in-Cuffs Show.

Many opinion-makers saw right through this strategy and asked the feds why they went after Stewart but not bigger fish? The stock price of Martha's company sagged but then recovered. People, especially women's groups, rallied around her. Instead of successfully exploiting Stewart because of her reputation as a tough woman, the prosecution, ironically, may have helped revive the feminist movement.

Politically motivated prosecutorial decision-making is not new. But when justice is served up on a platter of unfair biases against any group in society, it hurts the system. And it matters a lot, when the whole country is watching.

We need to ask whether we can tolerate this type of prosecutorial decision-making and in the meantime, we need to make it up to Martha, somehow, to send our own message of disgust for the way the government handled her case.

How should we make it up to Martha? For my part, I'm buying up Martha Stewart table linens and other kitchen stuff although I have absolutely no need for any of it. I'm even buying her magazine - though again, I have no intention of cooking a gourmet meal or growing a new variety of daisies or building a trellis to serve as a dramatic-but-tasteful backdrop for my garden. (I'm not even sure that my few scraggly perennials count as a garden.)

I'm not defending Martha because I'm a woman. Many men feel the same way, and body parts don't matter when you care about things like prosecutorial fairness. You don't have to be a Martha Stewart fan to want the feds to think twice before incarcerating anyone who committed a similar crime for nine months when so many criminals who committed far worse offenses are walking free.

Martha's been out of prison for a while, so we can't help her by complaining to the feds, but if it happens again, we can at least write a letter to our Congressmen and women, and to the President of the United States, saying something like: "I'm shocked that the government wasted my tax dollars sending this person to prison. All my friends agree with me, and we intend to vote for or against you in the next election based on what happens in this case."

Again: I'm not saying Stewart is innocent. There's no question she violated the law, and for that she had to pay a price. But people need to be punished for what they do, not for who they are, and the punishment should be proportionate, not gratuitous. Stewart should have paid a fine. Incarcerating her because it was the popular thing to do is craziness. Think of the Salem Witch Trials. Prosecutors and law enforcement officials were egged on by an anxious public that saw witches behind every bush. They, rounded up and prosecuted a group of people (mostly women) even executing twenty of them, to the general approval of the populace.

Couldn't happen today, you're thinking, right? Don't count on it. The fact is, prosecutors have a ton of power, and the public has very few options for holding them accountable when they abuse their authority. As I said in an earlier chapter, when it's a state prosecutor, you can mobilize people to prevent the reelection of a bad District Attorney and support a good one. But United States Attorneys are appointed, not elected, which means you have to think about who you are voting for in the presidential and congressional races in your district to have any power over the appointment of the chief federal prosecutor in your jurisdiction.

We need even more ideas, though, because the political process won't get us where we need to be. For one thing, elections don't work fast enough, and we can't afford to let a horrible prosecutor stay in office for years while we wait for a chance to vote for someone different. We need a way of influencing prosecutors' decisions while they are still in office, to prevent them from overdoing it, as with Martha

Stewart, or underdoing it, as with so many district attorneys who give plea bargains to child predators.

Court-watch programs are a recent innovation that help citizens hold prosecutors accountable. Individuals volunteer their time to sit in court and take notes about the actions of judges and lawyers. The information then gets logged into a database and is eventually reported to the public. These types of oversight groups can help inform the public about plea deals, and whether harsh enough charges are being filed in the first place. If decisions are unfair to victims, a court-watch group can launch a protest, or undertake a letter-writing campaign to the local media. For guidance about what a good court-watch program looks like, check out nationalfamilycourtwatchproject.org.

At the end of the day, it's about each of us playing a role in democracy by holding the government accountable for doing justice *fairly*. The job of prosecutor is not to put on a show for the nightly news by making fierce claims about bringing bad guys to justice. Nor should it be a job for politicians who want to use the high-profile position as a launch-pad to higher office. Doing justice fairly means making sure all criminals are prosecuted, including the rich and powerful, and that nobody is prosecuted purely for political gain.

Unless we work hard to make sure the right prosecutors get the job, we'll see unfair prosecutions over and over again. This time it was a celebrity - but next time it might be someone like you.

TWENTY-ONE

Suing the Victim

In 2005 Cyle Jones was convicted of sexually assaulting another student at the Groton-Dunstable High School in Massachusetts. After the criminal case was over, Jones's lawyer, Nelson P. Lovins, filed a lawsuit against the victim and her mother, claiming they violated Jones's civil rights and caused him emotional distress. How did a victim and her mother cause a *perpetrator* emotional distress, you wonder? By reporting the crime to police and speaking publicly about the assault. I'm not kidding. The lawsuit was eventually thrown out, and the lawyer was punished for bringing an unjust lawsuit, but can you believe the audacity of this sex offender and his attorney?

Does this make you crazy? It makes me crazy.

How about another example in the same vein? A group of parents in the town of Norfolk, Massachusetts were sued in 2006 when they protested a decision to allow four convicted sex offenders to live in a group home only steps away from families with small children. Parents in the neighborhood were terrified. They made the point, loudly, that this particular group home was supposed to house people with disabilities, not criminals, and certainly not convicted sex offenders. After much public outcry, the owner of the property moved the four sex offenders to another location. The families were thrilled that their children would be safe.

Happy ending, right? Wrong. The parents soon found themselves the targets of a vicious lawsuit, filed by David J. Apfel and Alisha R. Bloom of the Boston law firm Goodwin Procter LLP. These lawyers said the families violated the sex offenders' rights by complaining about them living in their neighborhood.

In both crazy cases, the sex offenders claimed they suffered from mental problems, and that as people with psychological issues, they were entitled to special rights under the Americans with Disabilities Act. It was a stunning assertion. (It still stuns me as I write about it today especially when I think about how the legal system treated Ruby McDonough, the woman I wrote about in an earlier chapter whose rights as a truly disabled person were completely ignored, and no big law firm showed up to help her!) These guys literally demanded that they be afforded special protection under civil rights laws – the same kinds of laws that helped stop widespread discrimination and violence against black citizens.

Think about that. Convicted sex offenders who brutalized little children claiming an entitlement to the *same special legal status* and civil rights protections as racial minorities.

If we can't discriminate against child rapists, who *can* we dislike openly without getting into legal trouble? Shouldn't we enthusiastically be heaping public scorn and loathing on people who rape children? Isn't anyone worried that giving free housing and food to child predators sends the wrong message? Before we start talking about convicted rapists as "disabled," shouldn't we use special laws, and give free housing, etc., to help the traumatized kids who are *truly disabled* because of the abuse they suffered at the hands of sex offenders?

Making sure child predators get a fair trial is a necessary and honorable thing to do. But there's nothing honorable about hurting innocent citizens by suing them for exercising their Constitutional right to report crime and testify in court. Defense attorneys who sue people for exercising their Constitutional rights are part of the reason people have so much disdain for criminal lawyers and for the legal system that allows them to sue innocent victims. When the public loses faith in the system, they start to take matters into their own hands.

Judging from the e-mails and letters I receive, the public is getting fed up. Even lawyers themselves are losing faith. In 2006, Jonathan Edington, a Connecticut attorney, killed his neighbor Barry James after Edington's wife told him that James had molested their two-year-old daughter.

As it turned out, the child had not been molested, but an awful lot of people sympathized with Edington because they understood his rage. No, Edington doesn't deserve a pass, and what he did was wrong. But there's something radically wrong when *lawyers* are becoming vigilantes.

On the off chance a sex offender is reading these pages, I have a word of advice: Beware. You may well pay the ultimate price at the hands of an outraged citizen fed up with a legal system that too often fails victims. Vigilantism is the kind of canary-in-a-coal-mine evidence that doesn't bode well for sex offenders, or for civility itself.

Lawyers for sex offenders should also be warned, and should stop fueling the fire in the belly of an angry public. Society is obviously at the end of its rope, and lawyers filing lawsuits to demand civil rights protections for "disabled" and "mentally ill" rapists could be responsible for severing the last thread that holds our social rope together.

Rapists aren't disabled or sick; they're criminals. And when these criminals falsely claim to be sick, they give the truly mentally ill a bad name. They may have compulsions, but so do many people, yet they don't act on them by hurting others. Defense lawyers say sex offenders should get special treatment because they can't help themselves. But if that were true, wouldn't they be doing all sorts of horrible things in public every day without regard for consequences? How come they always manage to commit their crimes in private, after careful planning, if it's all so "compulsive"?

There's no stronger compulsion than the urge to use the bathroom, yet sex offenders don't just pull down their pants in the middle of Main Street and use the double-yellow line as a toilet. If offenders can control their bathroom needs, they can control their impulse to rape children. And if they can't, they should be locked up *before* they hurt an innocent child, not placed in disabled housing, on the taxpayer's dime, next door to families, playgrounds and schoolchildren.

This issue shouldn't even be up for debate, but crazy ideas proliferate about sex offenders, in part, because a whole industry of "experts" makes a fortune testifying in criminal trials (usually at taxpayer expense) about the psychological needs of rapists. Relatively few experts, however, get paid to talk about the psychological needs of traumatized victims.

Is this twisted, or what? Who deserves to be comforted, the rapist, or the rapist's victim? Whose psychological well-being should we be more worried about - that of a convicted criminal who will feel sad if he can't get a reduced prison sentence, or that of a child victim who can't function in school because she can't stop shaking from the trauma of being raped? And who deserves to be sued - the rapist for committing his crime, or the victim for talking about it publicly?

The good news is, citizens are fighting back. They're not only successfully defending themselves against dumb lawsuits, they're using anti-SLAPP (Strategic Litigation Against Public Participation) laws to win sanctions against the lawyers who sue them for speaking out against child predators.

Initially designed to protect citizens from lawsuits meant to stop them from engaging in "public participation" activities, such as protesting chemical companies for dumping toxic waste in a local playground, anti-SLAPP laws allow protesters to dismiss those suits and win costs and sanctions against the lawyers who filed them.

Crime victims can use anti-SLAPP laws, too, when they engage in "public participation" activity such as calling the police, testifying in court and speaking publicly about crime.

Anti-SLAPP laws protect the Constitutionally protected petitioning rights of all citizens, including crime victims, though victims rarely know they have such rights, or how to use them. We need to do more to teach victims about anti-SLAPP laws.

I was the first lawyer in the country to use anti-SLAPP laws on behalf of crime victims. I helped a battered woman dismiss a lawsuit that had been filed against her by her husband after he was convicted of abusing her. He claimed she committed abuse of process and libel when she called the police and testified about his restraining order violations. I filed a motion under the anti-SLAPP law to dismiss his lawsuit, and we won a landmark decision that required the guy to pay a fine, as well as legal fees, as punishment for violating my client's Constitutional rights.

Today, many victims' rights lawyers use anti-SLAPP laws, but we need to spread the word because too many victims simply crumble in fear when a process server shows up at their door and hands them papers saying they're being sued for ten million dollars. They don't know how easy it is in many states to get the lawsuit dismissed, and get the people who filed it into a whole lot of trouble.

The ACLU often uses anti-SLAPP laws to defend, for free, people who are sued for exercising their free speech and protest rights, including sex offenders and child predators, but they usually refuse to help crime victims. I'm not sure why. If you get the chance, tell someone at the ACLU that you're going to start referring to them as the American CRIMINALS' Liberties Union.

The ACLU can't seem to accept the idea that the Constitution belongs to everyone - not just criminals. Until they get it straight, we need a privately funded ICLU (Innocent Citizens' Liberties Union), and we need to keep reminding the ACLU that the Constitution's purpose was to ensure liberty and justice for *all*, not some, including those who suffer, rather than commit, violent crimes.

If we work together, lawsuits against victims will stop overnight. Victims and innocent citizens have been taking a beating for too long. Now, hands raised, we're ready to SLAPP back!

TWENTY-TWO

Cleaning up the Dirt

The public has had its fill of lawyers who cheat, and judges who compound the suffering of the innocent.

When an attorney hides behind a license or a judge hides behind a robe as an excuse to behave badly, he or she should be shamed out of the system. The law is supposed to help promote civility, but when officers of the court act like idiots, civility suffers.

Part of the problem lies in the gap between our expectations and the sometimes-sordid realities of justice. Lawyers and judges do their thing in wood-paneled courtrooms, adorned with sepia-toned pictures of important looking men who are long dead. Pomp and circumstance practically oozes out of the walls. The high priests of the court speak Latin, cite cases from dusty law books, and utter multi-syllabic mumbo-jumbo like "heretofore the party of the first part," blah, blah, and blah. The judges sit wrapped in flowing black robes, delivering life-altering pronouncements from on high. For most people, this is awe-inspiring, and intimidating. So our expectations are raised, only to be dashed by a profoundly unjust outcome.

With more than a few bad apples in the profession, and an increasing degree of public exposure because of 24/7 news (alongside the public's insatiable appetite for all things controversial) judges and lawyers are on the hot seat in the court of public opinion like never before. Maybe the antiseptic light of publicity will serve as a kind of quality control device, and things will get better. I certainly hope so.

With so many lawyers and judges making the news for the horrible things they do, it's no wonder people pay little attention to the ones who are doing good work, and going out of their way to honor their profession. Many judges spend their nights and weekends teaching, talking to community groups, helping mentor new judges, and working with high school, college and law school students on mock trial competitions.

Many lawyers volunteer their time developing civilized justice systems in underdeveloped countries, or representing poor women who are forced to choose between being beaten by their husbands and homelessness. Lawyers regularly donate their time to provide free legal advice, and make house calls to draft wills for the elderly and disabled. In fact, the good deeds of lawyers are all over the place, but we don't see them because the bad apples are hogging all the (negative) attention.

As I mentioned in an earlier chapter, jokes about the legal system used to bug me, but not anymore. Joke away, American public, and don't show any new respect until the people in charge start getting it right.

What do I mean? The answer is not complicated. Getting it right means making sure that *justice*, not *winning*, is the name of the game. Getting it right means making sure lawyers who lie to get guilty criminals off are disbarred the first time they do it.

Getting it right means people must *not* become judges if they intend to use the power of the robe to promote a personal ideology that undermines the rule of law. We understand this when a new judge is appointed to the United States Supreme Court. We need to extend this concern to judges who preside over the cases that influence our daily lives, and directly affect our communities.

Getting it right means finding a way to make fighting for victims a financially manageable endeavor, instead of sending victims off to hunt for an inexperienced law student or pro bono lawyer. Most "victims' rights" organizations don't give a damn about victims anyway, but desperate people don't know any better so they'll take any lawyer they can get for free. We need more independent (not government) funding for excellent lawyers for victims; lawyers who know how to shake up the system and make sure those who have suffered at the hands of criminals are treated *at least as well* as the bad guys on trial. We spend millions of dollars every year helping obviously guilty murderers file frivolous appeals to challenge perfectly valid convictions. Wouldn't it make more sense to spend a little of that money to help victims whose rights are being violated with impunity because they don't even know they *have* rights?

I'm not suggesting we spend less on criminals' due process rights, but shouldn't we at least *try* to save a few bucks by heading off bogus legal proceedings and needless appeals? Couldn't we redirect a few of those precious dollars toward making the system a little fairer for victims?

Finally, getting it right means encouraging *all* lawyers to do more pro bono work, so that the profession as a whole rediscovers the importance of not always thinking about money. The role of judges and lawyers in society is far more important than that which can be measured by profit margins. Yes, lawyers have a right to make a living, even a good living, but we also have the capacity and the obligation to do *so much more.*

You can find lawyers willing to make life a little better for folks in every corner of this country, in small towns and big cities, in federal courtrooms and community centers. I do my part by representing victims for free. And I turn away many cases where I could make money, to make sure I have enough time for victims without means, because the *publicly funded* criminal justice system shouldn't cost an innocent crime victim a dime. Remember, the perpetrator often gets a publicly funded attorney, and his lawyer can use those funds to cause even *more* harm to the victim! The least we can do is help the victim fend off those tactics without sending her to the poorhouse, or forcing her to choose between justice and paying the rent.

Much of what I do for victims isn't easy, and some of it makes judges crazy. One judge hissed at me when I was giving a talk at a judicial training event. I asked a judge sitting nearby to slap her in the head for me. A grown-up judge hissing?!

The kind of work I do for victims isn't taught in law schools, which means there's never a form in the back of the law books to guide me when I'm writing a motion or filing a brief. Most of my clients have suffered Constitutional violations, but the criminal justice system isn't set up for victims to have their own voices in the courtroom, so I usually just create a path for them.

It's a fun challenge. I like making new law for victims, and filing motions nobody's ever seen before (e.g., "Motion to Sanction the Defense Attorney For Referring to the Victim as an 'Accuser' on the Grounds that the Prosecution – not the Victim – Filed the Charges 'Accusing' the Defendant of Rape"), but I always play by the rules. If I can't find a law that specifically applies to my client's situation, I cite the due process clause, or stomp my feet and cite "the inherent power of the court." Sometimes I have to file an appeal. Hell, I usually *want* to file an appeal, which means I'm hoping the trial court will rule against me so that I *can* file an appeal because if I win at the trial level, I only help that one victim in that one case. If I win on appeal, the decision applies to all victims.

I understand that the criminal justice system is not supposed to be a day at the beach for victims. But it's not supposed to feel like a day on the battlefields of Afghanistan, either. When bad things happen needlessly to law-abiding citizens, it's not only about that one person feeling gypped or violated or uncomfortable. It's about an entire system malfunctioning, and it's about the audacity of the people in charge calling it "justice." The reputation of our legal system has been faltering since the O.J. Simpson trial, and unless major changes are implemented soon, respect for the rule of law itself will soon fade. This is unacceptable for a nation that prides itself as a world leader, whose government is founded on principles of fundamental respect for the rights of *all* citizens, not just criminals.

The law as an institution is far more important than any single person, lawyer, judge or corporation. When the law works the way it should, it inspires mutual respect and human decency. When it fails, we lose the value of these essential ideals, which is why we have a right - no, a *duty* - to complain when injustice happens. Scream! Throw things! Make as much noise as possible until the people in charge start listening. Run for office if you can, or start a campaign to showcase the problems in your community by running ads in local papers. Better yet, use Facebook or Twitter to get the word out – just do something! You know the old saying, if you're not part of the solution, you're part of the problem.

This book has given you a few ideas about how to make things better, but it is not at all the final word on what we need to do to fix what's broken. You, the reader, have to come up with your own ideas. You have to find and join forces with like-minded others to demand change because there is great power in numbers.

Use the Internet to communicate and brainstorm with people around the country who share your concerns. Create a volunteer group in your neighborhood. Give money to worthy foundations that are doing meaningful work. Put ads in local papers. Sponsor community education events, and get yourself on local or national television to talk about the injustices that you see.

Contact elected officials. Organize a rally. Write letters to judges. Submit op-eds to newspapers. Make a protest sign and stand in front of your state house, courthouse, or town hall every day until someone pays attention.

As I've said to many, many audiences comprised of angry citizens who are fed up: Do *anything you can*! Do not wait for a disaster, and don't expect an invitation. Inject yourself into the process, demand a seat at the table, let your voice be heard, and do not stop speaking until you are satisfied. If we all do this, every time we see an injustice, there's a good chance we would finally start to see justice for all!

ACKNOWLEDGEMENTS

Writing this book was hard but figuring out whom to name in the acknowledgments section was impossible. Thus, at the risk of sounding philosophical about who deserves recognition for being an inspirational "part" of this book, I am opting for the all-inclusive "you know who you are" technique - with special attention to my dad who has never learned how to be mean and doesn't understand meanness in others, and to my five incredible children. Each of them suffered, and I hope will someday benefit, not only because of what it took to write this book but also because of the way my lifetime commitment to justice for crime victims has deprived them of my attention. I am the luckiest mother on earth that they turned out to be such wonderful people.

I'm grateful to my dear friend Norman Knight who stands alone in his capacity to give and love generously, without expectation, simply because it matters. Just thinking about him makes me feel inspired to help others.

I also appreciate the people who read this book in its various stages and offered helpful comments. They all gave time they didn't have. Judge Roderick Kennedy found a way to use poetry to nudge me away from excessive hyperbole and my sister Barbara, one of the busiest and most dedicated mothers I know, managed to read it and give good advice between carpools, doctor visits and helping her children get pudding out of the dog's ear.

A special note of thanks to Bill O'Reilly, a particularly good man. His support for more than fifteen years has made all the difference. We don't agree about everything, but we share a commitment to the protection of children and an abiding faith that Americans, like no other culture, can transcend political differences in a common quest for a better society.

Pundits and talk show hosts are a funny breed. People take us seriously, and I never say something on television that I don't believe is true (though I might ham it up a little for effect). But let me let you in on a little secret: We know that ratings matter, and we know what "works" on television. This doesn't mean we're not sincere, but it means you're only getting a slice of who we really are when you hear us pontificating about an issue. I wish I could use my airtime to tell you about all the things that I fight for - all the cases my students and I volunteer to work on when nobody is looking that raise important issues about justice and fair treatment for victimized women, men and children. But I don't own a network.

Even this book is but a slice of the pie, and issues worthy of attention are not covered. I apologize for that. For example, the family court system is a mess, and I hear horrifying stories every day, mostly from mothers like Wendy Titelman, who love their children more than life itself, but were ordered by a judge to have no contact with them as punishment for speaking out about abuse. I could have written an entire book on the corruption and dirty tricks in our family courts and the deranged judges who let it happen.

And I could have written reams about the atrocities in the world of child protective services. I can't even keep up with the calls I get about children "falling through the cracks," some literally dying while under the care of a state agency. Many social workers are overworked and underpaid, but the problems run deeper than that. All the money in the world didn't help little Haleigh Poutre, a Massachusetts child who nearly died in 2005 after being beaten by her adoptive mother. Social services received more than a dozen reports of abuse but did nothing because they were told the child was self-abusive. I'm not a trained social worker but isn't that exactly what abusive parents say when they're trying not to get caught?

I limited this book's scope to the criminal justice system, and, even then, I had to leave many things out. So I want to hear what you think about what's in here and what's missing. Tell me about the injustices that matter to you, and let's work together to build a better legal system that not only promises, but truly delivers, *Justice for All*.

ABOUT THE AUTHOR

WENDY MURPHY represents victims of violent crime in civil and criminal litigation and is an adjunct professor at New England Law | Boston, where she teaches an advanced seminar on sexual violence and the criminal justice system. She served as a visiting scholar at Harvard Law School and is a former Massachusetts prosecutor who specialized in child abuse and sex crimes. Together with the Fox News Channel's Bill O'Reilly, she is fighting for mandatory sentencing laws for child sex offenders in all fifty states. She has provided legal analysis for all the major networks and cable news channels, and lives outside Boston with her husband and five children.

31996384R00154

Made in the USA
Lexington, KY
02 May 2014